Desserts

A Pyramid Cookery Paperback

Desserts

hamlyn

An Hachette Livre UK Company

A Pyramid Paperback

First published in Great Britain in 2008 by
Hamlyn, a division of Octopus Publishing Group Ltd
2–4 Heron Quays, London E14 4JP
www.octopusbooks.co.uk

ISBN 978-0-600-61808-9

A CIP catalogue record for this book is available from the British Library

Printed and bound in China

10 9 8 7 6 5 4 3 2 1

Both metric and imperial measurements
are given for the recipes. Use one set of
measures only, not a mixture of both.

Ovens should be preheated to the specified
temperature. If using a fan-assisted oven,
follow the manufacturer's instructions for
adjusting the time and temperature. Grills
should also be preheated.

This book includes dishes made with nuts
and nut derivatives. It is advisable for
those with known allergic reactions to
nuts and nut derivatives and those who
may be potentially vulnerable to these
allergies, such as pregnant and nursing
mothers, invalids, the elderly, babies and
children, to avoid dishes made with nuts
and nut oils. It is also prudent to check
the labels of prepreared ingredients for
the possible inclusion of nut derivatives.

Contents

Introduction

Many people consider the dessert course to be the most anticipated part of a meal. There is such a vast array of choices for those with a sweet tooth that it can often be difficult to decide just what you fancy to round off a delicious dinner. For the keen cook, dessert presents the opportunity to show off your creative leanings. A good dessert should complement the previous courses and provide a satisfactory finish to a meal. With this in mind, you need to consider whether to prepare something very light and simple or whether your guests can handle a deliciously rich, indulgent pudding.

Throughout this book you will discover recipes that cover every conceivable dessert, from summery sorbets to warming wintery puds, and from fruit flans to treats for serious chocoholics. There are also tips for pastry making and cake decoration, as well as advice on equipment and storage. With this book in your recipe collection, you will have everything you need to create the perfect dessert for every occasion.

PASTRY PERFECTION

If you are a dessert fan, you'll need to perfect the art of pastry making. While ready-made pastry is perfectly acceptable for many sweet pies and flans and can be a bit of a life-saver when time is running short, nothing quite beats the real thing. Many people assume that making your own pastry is fiddly and time consuming, yet a basic shortcrust pastry can be prepared in a matter of minutes and can be made well in advance. It's also extremely versatile and can be frozen, so you can make a big batch and freeze it in portions ready for future use.

Hot and cold

If you stick to a few basic rules you should turn out perfect pastry every time. One of the most important things to remember is that pastry needs to be kept cool and doesn't like to be handled too much. If you are making a pastry that requires a number of rolling steps, keep it in the fridge in between to ensure it stays chilled. Any liquid you add to the

ingredients should always be cold. This chilly side to the preparation is counteracted by the fact that pastry should always be cooked in a hot oven for the best results. Make sure your oven has reached the required temperature before cooking and try to resist the temptation of continually opening the door to check on the pastry's progress.

Blind baking

Many flan, pie and tart dishes require the pastry case to be blind baked first. All this basically means is that you give the pastry a bit of a head start by cooking it for a while without the filling. If you are going to be using this technique frequently, buy some ceramic baking beans. However, any dried peas or beans, or rice, will do the trick. These act as a weight so that the pastry doesn't rise or bubble. Simply line the pastry case with greaseproof paper, tip in the beans and cook for the specified time.

Types of pastry

There are a number of different types of pastry that you will find throughout the book, which are used in numerous dessert recipes. Here is a brief description of the more commonly used types.

SHORTCRUST: This is certainly the most widely used pastry when it comes to desserts. It has a crumbly texture and sweet flavour making it ideal for all sweet flans and tarts. (See recipe on page 70.)

PUFF: This pastry is as light as a feather and has a satisfying, crispy finish. The beauty of it lies in the fact that it is rich and buttery without being overly heavy or filling. It is often used to make decadent cream-filled cakes and desserts. While puff pastry is more complicated and time consuming to make than shortcrust, the results more than justify the effort involved.

FLAKY: Like puff pastry, the method for this involves rolling and folding the dough to create light, flaky layers. The more even these are the better the results.

CHOUX: This is a paste that is made from flour, butter, eggs, water and sugar. It is most famously used for those naughty-but-nice treats - profiteroles and éclairs. There's a bit of a knack to making perfect choux pastry, but once you've mastered it you'll be knocking up batches of it in no time.

KEEPING COOL

With a whole chapter dedicated to 'Ices and cold desserts', it is easy to see that ice creams and sorbets are very popular when it comes to finishing a meal. A simple fruit sorbet can be the perfect complement to a rich, hearty main course, while ice cream can be served on its own or as an accompaniment to virtually any hot or cold sweet pie or torte. Chilled desserts are ideal for dinner parties as they can be prepared in advance and removed from the freezer a few minutes before serving.

so that the ice crystals break up and the finished result is smooth and creamy with an even texture.

CHOCOLATE HEAVEN

It is impossible to talk about desserts without mentioning chocolate and recipes for chocolate desserts appear in all of the chapters in this book. It is such a widely loved and versatile ingredient that chocolate puds are always a popular choice and this book gives you something to suit every mood, whether you fancy something hot or cold, simple or decadent.

The most important thing to bear in mind when cooking with chocolate is to choose a really good-quality product as this will be reflected in the finished dish. In chocolate terms, this means a high cocoa content and 70 per cent or above is ideal.

Ice creams and sorbets

Ice cream is basically a frozen custard made from cream or eggs and sugar, combined with fruit or another main flavouring ingredient. Sorbets and granitas have a much lighter consistency and these are usually a fairly simple combination of sugar, water and fruit. Sorbets have a velvety smooth texture, whereas granitas have large crystals and a rougher consistency.

Ice cream makers

If you have a soft spot for iced desserts and plan on making them regularly, you might consider investing in an ice cream machine. It will produce a more uniform, velvety texture and also removes some of the preparation work. However, they are by no means essential and you can create wonderful homemade ice creams and sorbets by hand. The key is to keep stirring the mixture as it's chilling and freezing

Melting chocolate

This is an easy technique that is required for numerous recipes. Plain chocolate is easier to melt than milk as it has a lower fat content and burns less easily. When working with either you need to keep to a gentle heat and use minimal stirring.

ON THE HOB: Break the chocolate into pieces and put them in a heatproof bowl. Rest the bowl over a pan of gently simmering water, making sure that the base of the bowl cannot come into contact with the water. Once the chocolate starts to melt, turn off the heat and leave it until it is completely melted, stirring once or twice until no lumps remain. It's crucial that no water gets into the bowl while the chocolate is melting as this will make the chocolate solidify. Use the melted chocolate immediately. It will stay soft if you keep it in a warm place while you are working with it.

IN THE MICROWAVE: Use a microwave-proof bowl and melt the chocolate on a medium power setting in one-minute spurts, checking the chocolate frequently.

IN THE OVEN: Put the chocolate in a small ovenproof bowl or dish and leave the bowl in a low oven, 110°C (225°F), Gas Mark ¼, checking frequently. Alternatively, place the bowl in an oven that has been switched off after being used for baking.

Chocolate curls

These can be simply made by running a swivel vegetable peeler along the smooth underside of a bar of plain dark (or white) chocolate. If the curls are very tiny, microwave the bar of chocolate in 15-second bursts until it softens and you can make bigger curls.

Chocolate scribbles

Line a tray with nonstick baking paper. Fill a paper piping bag with a little melted chocolate and snip off a tiny tip. 'Draw' shapes on the paper – scribbled lines, curvy swirls or filigree patterns – and leave them to set. Peel the paper away and use the scribbles to decorate chilled desserts. Don't make the patterns too delicate or they will break.

USING FRUIT

Like chocolate, fruit is another important ingredient in the world of desserts. Whole fruits are baked (Baked Saffron Peaches with Mango and Cream, page 90) or poached (Cranberry Poached Pears, page 97); berries are made into coulis, sauces, and cake fillings; smaller fruits are crystallized and used to decorate cakes; and citrus rind is used as both decoration and flavouring. There is a whole chapter in the book dedicated to fruit desserts and you will find examples of all these incarnations there. Fruit works incredibly well in dessert recipes as most varieties have a naturally sweet flavour and can be combined with ingredients, such as cream or chocolate, to produce mouthwatering results.

Citrus swirls

Orange or lemon swirls make really beautiful cake decorations and they are easy to make. Use a parer to remove thin strips of rind from the orange or lemon – try to make these as long as possible. Next, carefully wind each strip around a straw or chopstick. Hold the swirl in place and leave it for a few minutes, until the moisture from the rind begins to dry out so the swirl keeps its shape. Pull the swirls off the straw and use for decoration.

Fruit syrup

You can experiment with all kinds of fruit to make syrups. They are wonderful served with ice cream or drizzled over cakes or other desserts. Small fruits such as blackberries and raspberries are ideal for making fruit syrups. As a rough guide, use about 300 g (10 oz) fruit, 400 g (13 oz) caster sugar and 150 ml (¼ pint) water. Heat the ingredients in a pan until the sugar has melted, then bring to the boil and cook for about 10 minutes, stirring frequently. Turn off the heat and pour the liquid through a sieve to collect the syrup. Allow to cool, then use as required.

Ices and cold desserts

Peppermint candy ice cream

Preparation time **20 minutes**,
   plus freezing
Cooking time **5 minutes**
Serves **4**

50 g (2 oz) peppermint candy canes
   or peppermint rock
4 egg yolks
50 g (2 oz) caster sugar
1 teaspoon cornflour
300 ml (½ pint) milk
300 ml (½ pint) whipping cream
extra crushed peppermint candy or
   peppermint rock, to decorate
   (optional)

1 Put the candy canes or rock into a polythene bag and then beat with the end of a rolling pin until roughly crushed. Continue to beat until the candy is broken into small granules.

2 Beat the egg yolks in a bowl with the sugar, cornflour and a little of the milk until smooth. Bring the remaining milk to the boil in a heavy-based saucepan. Pour the milk over the egg yolk mixture, whisking well until combined. Return the mixture to the saucepan and cook very gently, stirring until it has thickened enough to coat the back of the spoon thinly.

3 Transfer the custard to a bowl, cover with a circle of greaseproof paper to prevent a skin from forming and leave to cool. Chill in the refrigerator until very cold.*

4 Lightly whip the cream and fold it into the custard with the crushed candy. Turn into a freezer container, cover and freeze until the mixture has frozen around the edges. Transfer to a bowl and whisk lightly.

5 Return to the freezer until the mixture has once again frozen around the edges. Repeat the whisking and freezing once or twice more, then freeze the ice cream until ready to serve.

6 Transfer the ice cream to the refrigerator for about 30 minutes before serving to soften slightly. Scoop the ice cream into glasses and sprinkle with extra crushed peppermint candy, if you like.

* If using an ice cream machine, follow the recipe until the end of step 3. Transfer the custard to the machine and add the cream. Churn and freeze following the manufacturer's instructions. Follow the serving suggestion at the end of step 6.

Peach ice cream

Preparation time **20 minutes**,
   plus cooling and freezing
Cooking time **15 minutes**
Serves **6–8**

4 large, ripe peaches, total weight
   about 750 g (1½ lb), skinned
50 g (2 oz) icing sugar
1 tablespoon lemon juice
2 tablespoons white wine
2 teaspoons gelatine
4 egg yolks
300 ml (½ pint) double cream
waffle cones dipped in melted
   chocolate and pistachios, to serve

1 Purée the peach flesh with the sugar in a blender or
food processor. Mix together the lemon juice and wine
in a small bowl and sprinkle on the gelatine.

2 Transfer the peach purée to a large heatproof bowl.
Beat in the egg yolks. Place the bowl over a pan of
gently simmering water and stir until the mixture
has thickened.

3 Put the bowl of gelatine mixture into a shallow pan of
hot water and leave until it dissolves. Stir the gelatine
into the peach mixture and leave to cool.*

4 Whip the cream until it forms soft peaks, then fold it
into the peach mixture.

5 Transfer it to a freezer container, cover and freeze
until firm, beating twice at hourly intervals. Serve with
waffle cones dipped in melted plain dark chocolate and
crushed pistachio nuts.

* If using an ice cream machine, follow the recipe until the end of step 3. Pour
the mixture into the machine and add the cream. Churn and freeze following
the manufacturer's instructions. Follow the serving suggestion at the end of
step 5.

Old-fashioned vanilla ice cream with hot caramel sauce

Preparation time **10 minutes**,
    plus cooling and freezing
Cooking time **25 minutes**
Serves **6**

300 ml (½ pint) single cream
1 vanilla pod
4 egg yolks
50 g (2 oz) caster sugar
300 ml (½ pint) double or
    whipping cream
redcurrants coated in icing sugar,
    to serve (optional)

Caramel sauce
200 ml (7 fl oz) water
75 g (3 oz) caster sugar
juice of ½ lemon

1 Put the single cream and vanilla pod into a heavy-based saucepan, set over a low heat and bring to just below boiling. Remove from the heat and leave to infuse.

2 Place the egg yolks and sugar into a heatproof bowl and set over a pan of gently simmering water. Stir with a wooden spoon until thick and creamy, then gradually stir in the scalded single cream, removing the vanilla pod. Continue stirring for 15 minutes until the custard coats the spoon. Remove the bowl from the heat and cool.*

3 Pour the vanilla mixture into a freezer container, cover and transfer to the freezer for about 45 minutes or until slushy. Whip the cream until it just holds its shape. Remove the vanilla mixture from the freezer, beat thoroughly, then fold in the cream. Return the mixture to the container, cover and freeze for a further 45 minutes, then beat again until smooth. Freeze the ice cream for 1–2 hours.

4 To make the caramel sauce, pour 150 ml (¼ pint) of the water into a heavy-based saucepan and add the sugar. Heat gently until the sugar has dissolved. Increase the heat and cook rapidly until the syrup begins to caramelize. The temperature will register 180°C (350°F) on a sugar thermometer – caramel stage. Remove from the heat and gradually stir in the remaining water with the lemon juice. Leave to cool, then gently reheat the sauce before serving.

5 Transfer the ice cream to the refrigerator for about 30 minutes to soften slightly before serving. Decorate with redcurrants coated in icing sugar and hot caramel sauce.

* If using an ice cream machine, follow the recipe until the end of step 2. Pour the mixture into the machine and add the cream. Churn and freeze following the manufacturer's instructions. Follow the serving suggestion at the end of step 5.

Chocolate chip ice cream

Preparation time **15 minutes**,
  plus cooling and freezing
Cooking time **15 minutes**
Serves **4–6**

300 ml (½ pint) milk
75 g (3 oz) soft dark brown sugar
75 g (3 oz) plain dark chocolate,
  broken into pieces
2 eggs, beaten
½ teaspoon vanilla extract
300 ml (½ pint) double cream
75 g (3 oz) chocolate chips
mini chocolate cookies, to serve
  (optional)

1 Put the milk, sugar and chocolate into a saucepan and heat gently until the chocolate has melted and the sugar dissolved. Pour the warm mixture on to the beaten eggs, stirring constantly.

2 Return the mixture to the pan and cook over a low heat, stirring constantly, until the custard thickens very slightly. Strain the mixture into a bowl and add the vanilla extract. Leave to cool.*

3 Whip the cream until it forms soft peaks, then whisk it into the cooled custard.

4 Stir in the chocolate chips. Turn the mixture into a freezer container, cover and freeze until firm.

5 About 30 minutes before serving, transfer the ice cream to the refrigerator to soften. Spoon or scoop the ice cream into individual dishes and serve with mini chocolate cookies.

* If using an ice cream machine, follow the recipe until the end of step 2. Pour the mixture into the machine and add the cream. Churn and freeze following the manufacturer's instructions. Once frozen, fold in the chocolate chips. Follow the serving suggestion at the end of step 5.

Lavender honey ice cream with roasted figs

Preparation time **20 minutes**,
  plus chilling and freezing
Cooking time **15 minutes**
Serves **4**

6 tablespoons lavender honey (or
  mild flower honey plus flowers
  from 8 lavender sprigs)
4 egg yolks
1 teaspoon cornflour
1 tablespoon caster sugar
300 ml (½ pint) milk
300 ml (½ pint) whipping cream
lavender sprigs, to decorate
  (optional)

Roasted figs
4 large fresh figs
2 tablespoons clear honey
1 tablespoon fresh orange juice

1 Put the honey, egg yolks, cornflour and sugar into a bowl and whisk lightly to combine. Bring the milk to the boil in a heavy-based saucepan. Pour the milk over the egg yolk mixture, whisking well until combined. Return the mixture to the saucepan and cook very gently, stirring constantly, until the custard has thickened enough to coat the back of the spoon thinly. Transfer to a bowl and cover with a circle of greaseproof paper to prevent a skin from forming. Leave to cool, then chill in the refrigerator until very cold.*

2 Lightly whip the cream and gently fold it into the custard (with the lavender flowers if using mild flower honey). Turn the mixture into a freezer container, cover and freeze until it has frozen around the edges. Transfer to a bowl and whisk lightly. Refreeze until the mixture has once again frozen around the edges. Repeat the whisking and freezing once or twice more.

3 Meanwhile, to cook the figs, cut a cross in the top of each one and place in a shallow ovenproof dish. Brush the figs with the honey and drizzle with the orange juice. Roast in a preheated oven, 220°C (425°F), Gas Mark 7, for about 10 minutes until lightly caramelized around the edges.

4 To serve, transfer the ice cream to the refrigerator 30 minutes before serving, to soften slightly. Scoop into serving glasses with the figs, spooning over any juices. Decorate with lavender sprigs if you like.

* If using an ice cream machine, follow the recipe until the end of step 1. Pour the mixture into the machine and add the cream. Churn and freeze following the manufacturer's instructions. Follow the serving suggestion at the end of step 4.

Honeyed banana ice cream with nuts

Preparation time **15 minutes**,
  plus freezing
Serves **4–6**

500 g (1 lb) bananas, peeled
2 tablespoons lemon juice
3 tablespoons thick honey
150 ml (¼ pint) natural yogurt
50 g (2 oz) chopped nuts
150 ml (¼ pint) double cream
2 egg whites

Pralines
120 ml (4 fl oz) water
175 g (6 oz) caster sugar
2 tablespoons golden syrup
175 g (6 oz) toasted almonds

1 Put the bananas into a bowl with the lemon juice and mash until smooth. Stir in the honey, then the yogurt and nuts and beat well.

2 Whip the cream until it forms soft peaks and fold into the banana mixture.* Transfer the mixture to a freezer container, cover and freeze until partially set.

3 Whisk the egg whites until stiff. Beat the banana mixture to break up the ice crystals, then fold in the egg whites and freeze until firm.

4 To make the pralines, pour the water into a heavy-based saucepan and add the caster sugar and golden syrup. Simmer gently until the sugar has dissolved to make a caramel syrup. Place the toasted almonds on a lightly oiled piece of foil and pour the syrup over. Let set for 1 hour. Once set, break up into irregular pieces and serve with the ice cream.

* If using an ice cream machine, follow the recipe until midway through step 2. Transfer the banana mixture to the ice cream machine and churn and freeze until half frozen. Whisk the egg whites until they form soft peaks, then add to the half-frozen mixture. Continue to freeze until completely frozen. Follow the serving suggestion in step 4.

Apricot and Amaretto ice cream with warm toffee sauce

Preparation time **20 minutes**,
plus cooling and freezing
Cooking time **25 minutes**
Serves **4**

250 g (8 oz) ready-to-eat
dried apricots
2 tablespoons Amaretto di Saronno
150 ml (¼ pint) double or
whipping cream
125 g (4 oz) granulated sugar
150 ml (¼ pint) water
2 egg whites
amaretti biscuits, to serve (optional)

Warm toffee sauce
75 g (3 oz) butter
1 tablespoon golden syrup
75 g (3 oz) brown sugar
4 tablespoons evaporated milk

1 Place the apricots in a saucepan and cover with cold water. Cover the pan and simmer gently for 15 minutes or until soft.

2 Drain the apricots, transfer to a food processor or blender and process to a purée. Leave to cool, then transfer to a medium bowl and stir in the liqueur. Whip the cream until it forms soft peaks, then gently fold it into the apricot purée.

3 Place the sugar and water in a heavy-based pan and heat gently until the sugar dissolves, stirring all the time, then boil, until the syrup registers 120°C (250°F) on a sugar thermometer – hard ball stage.

4 Meanwhile, put the egg whites into a bowl and beat until stiff. Slowly pour on the boiling syrup, beating the egg whites at high speed all the time and continuing to beat until cool.

5 Combine the apricot mixture and the egg white mixture together, mixing well. Transfer the mixture to a freezer container, cover and freeze until firm without further beating.*

6 To make the toffee sauce, place all the ingredients in a heavy-based saucepan and heat gently, stirring constantly with a wooden spoon, until the sugar has dissolved. Bring to the boil, then remove the pan from the heat.

7 Serve the ice cream with amaretti biscuits and the warm toffee sauce.

* Please note that there is no need to make this ice cream in an ice cream machine.

Strawberry ice cream with strawberry syrup

Preparation time **15 minutes**,
  plus freezing
Serves **6**

500 g (1 lb) strawberries, hulled
4 tablespoons fresh orange juice
175 g (6 oz) caster sugar
450 ml (¾ pint) whipping cream
wild strawberries, to decorate

Strawberry syrup
2 tablespoons water
2 tablespoons honey
50 g (2 oz) strawberries

1 Finely mash the strawberries and mix with the orange juice to form a smooth purée. Stir in the sugar.*

2 Whip the cream until it forms soft peaks and fold into the purée. Pour the mixture into a 1 kg (2 lb) loaf tin. Freeze for 1½ hours or until partly frozen.

3 Turn the mixture into a bowl, break it up with a fork and then whisk until smooth. Return the mixture to the loaf tin and freeze for at least 5 hours until it is completely frozen.

4 To make the strawberry syrup, pour the water into a heavy-based saucepan and then add the honey and strawberries. Heat until boiling, then pour through a wire-mesh strainer. Discard the fruit and pour the syrup over the ice cream.

5 Transfer the ice cream to the refrigerator 30 minutes before serving, to soften. Decorate with some wild strawberries and strawberry syrup.

* If using an ice cream machine, follow the recipe until the end of step 1. Place the mixture in the machine and add the cream. Churn and freeze following the manufacturer's instructions. Serve with strawberries and syrup.

Summer berry sorbet

Preparation time **5 minutes**,
   plus freezing
Serves **2**

250 g (8 oz) frozen mixed
   summer berries
75 ml (3 fl oz) spiced berry cordial
2 tablespoons Kirsch or vodka
1 tablespoon fresh lime juice

1 Chill a shallow freezer container.* Put the berries, cordial, Kirsch or vodka, and lime juice into a food processor or blender and purée until smooth. Do not overprocess, as this will soften the mixture too much.

2 Turn the purée into the chilled container, cover and freeze for at least 25 minutes. Spoon the sorbet into bowls and serve.

* Please note that there is no need to make
this sorbet in an ice cream machine.

Apricot and orange sorbet

Preparation time **20 minutes**,
  plus cooling and freezing
Cooking time **8 minutes**
Serves **6–8**

150 g (5 oz) caster sugar
300 ml (½ pint) water
75 ml (3 fl oz) fresh orange juice
3 tablespoons fresh lemon juice
grated rind of 1 orange
500 g (1 lb) ripe apricots, halved
  and pitted
1 egg white
sugared mint strips, to decorate
  (optional)

1 Put the sugar, water, orange and lemon juices and orange rind into a saucepan and bring to the boil, stirring until the sugar has dissolved. Increase the heat and boil rapidly for about 5 minutes until the syrup registers 110°C (225°F) on a sugar thermometer – thread stage. Add the apricots and simmer gently for about 2 minutes until they have softened slightly. Leave them to cool in the syrup.

2 Pour the fruit and syrup into a food processor or blender and process to a smooth purée.* Pour into a freezer container, cover and freeze for about 2 hours until frozen around the sides but slushy in the centre.

3 Tip the frozen syrup into a bowl and whisk briefly until smooth. Whisk the egg white until it forms soft peaks and fold into the fruit using a metal spoon. Pour the mixture back into the container and freeze for about 6 hours.

4 Transfer the sorbet to the refrigerator about 20 minutes before serving to soften slightly. To serve, arrange scoops of sorbet in individual glasses and decorate with sugared mint strips, if liked.

* If using an ice cream machine, follow the recipe until midway through step 2. Then pour into the machine and freeze until half-frozen. Whisk the egg whites until they form soft peaks and add to the half-frozen mixture. Continue to freeze until completely frozen. Follow the serving suggestion at the end of step 4.

Fresh melon sorbet

Preparation time **15 minutes**,
 plus freezing
Serves **4–6**

1 cantaloupe melon (or honeydew
 or watermelon), weighing
 1 kg (2 lb)
50 g (2 oz) icing sugar
juice of 1 lime or small lemon
1 egg white

1 Cut the melon in half and scoop out and discard the seeds. Scoop out the melon flesh with a spoon and discard the shells.

2 Place the flesh in a food processor or blender with the icing sugar and lime or lemon juice. Process to a purée,* then pour into a freezer container, cover and freeze for 2–3 hours.

3 Whisk the melon mixture to break up the ice crystals. Whisk the egg white until stiff, then whisk it into the half-frozen melon mixture. Return to the freezer and leave until firm.

4 Transfer the sorbet to the refrigerator 20 minutes before serving to soften slightly. Scoop the sorbet into glass dishes to serve.

* If using an ice cream machine, follow the recipe until midway through step 2. Pour into the machine and churn and freeze until half-frozen. Whisk the egg whites until they form soft peaks and add to the machine. Continue to freeze until completely frozen. Serve in glass dishes.

Tangy lemon sorbet

Preparation time **15 minutes**,
   plus cooling and freezing
Cooking time **10–15 minutes**
Serves **4–6**

600 ml (1 pint) water
250 g (8 oz) granulated sugar
3 tablespoons water
3 teaspoons gelatine
rind of 2 lemons
300 ml (½ pint) fresh lemon juice
2 egg whites

Candied lemon peel

120 ml (4 fl oz) water
115 g (4 oz) caster sugar, plus extra
   for sprinkling
peel of 1 large lemon, finely
   chopped

1 Put the 600 ml (1 pint) of water and the sugar into a small pan and heat gently until the sugar dissolves. Bring to the boil and boil steadily for 10 minutes. Leave to cool.

2 Put the 3 tablespoons of water in a small bowl and sprinkle on the gelatine. Set the bowl over a pan of simmering water and leave until the gelatine goes spongy. Whisk the gelatine mixture into the syrup with the lemon rind and juice.*

3 Pour the lemon mixture into a freezer container, cover and freeze for about 1 hour until partially frozen. Turn the partially frozen mixture into a chilled bowl and beat lightly to break up the crystals.

4 Whisk the egg whites until stiff and carefully fold into the lemon mixture. Freeze for a further 1½ hours, then whisk again and freeze until firm.

5 To make the candied lemon peel, pour the water into a heavy-based saucepan and add the caster sugar. Add the peel and heat gently until the sugar dissolves and has turned into a light syrup. Remove from the heat, drain the peel, and coat with a little extra sugar.

6 To serve, decorate the sorbet with candied lemon peel.

* If using an ice cream machine, follow the recipe until the end of step 2. Pour the mixture into the machine and churn and freeze until half-frozen. Whisk the egg whites until they form soft peaks and add to the half-frozen mixture. Freeze again until completely frozen. Serve with candied lemon peel.

Coffee granita

Preparation time **10 minutes**,
  plus cooling and freezing
Serves **4**

4 tablespoons freshly ground
  strong coffee
125 g (4 oz) caster sugar
450 ml (¾ pint) boiling water
whipped cream, to serve (optional)

1 Put the ground coffee and sugar into a jug and stir in the boiling water. Stir until the sugar has dissolved, then leave to cool.*

2 Strain the coffee liquid into a freezer container, cover and chill in the refrigerator for about 30 minutes. Transfer to the freezer and freeze for at least 2 hours or until completely solid.

3 Remove the granita from the container, then quickly chop it into large chunks with a large strong knife. Return it to the container and freeze again until required. Serve straight from the freezer, with whipped cream if you like.

* Please note that granitas should not be made in an ice cream machine.

Champagne water ice

Preparation time **15 minutes**,
plus cooling and freezing
Cooking time **5–10 minutes**
Serves **6**

250 g (8 oz) sugar
300 ml (½ pint) water
300 ml (½ pint) Champagne
juice of 1 lemon and 1 orange
strawberries, to serve

1 Put the sugar and water into a heavy-based saucepan and heat until the sugar has dissolved.

2 Stir the Champagne and fruit juices into the sugar syrup,* then pour into a shallow container and freeze. When the mixture is frozen around the edges, but soft in the centre, tip it into a food processor and process until smooth. Return it to the container and refreeze.

3 Repeat the whisking at intervals until the ice is creamy, smooth and white. Serve with strawberries.

* If using an ice cream machine, follow the recipe until midway through step 2. Then pour the mixture into the machine and churn and freeze. Serve with strawberries.

Peppered panna cotta with strawberry sauce

Preparation time **20 minutes**,
plus setting
Cooking time **3 minutes**
Serves **6**

1 teaspoon pink peppercorns
in brine
1 teaspoon powdered gelatine
2 tablespoons water
250 g (8 oz) mascarpone cheese
300 ml (½ pint) double cream
150 g (5 oz) white chocolate,
chopped
300 g (10 oz) strawberries
2–3 tablespoons icing sugar

To decorate
piped chocolate scribbles (see
page 10)
fresh strawberries

1 Rinse and dry the peppercorns. Use a pestle and mortar to crush them until they are fairly finely ground. Sprinkle the gelatine over the water in a small bowl and leave it to stand for 5 minutes. Lightly oil 6 125 ml (4 fl oz) dariole moulds.

2 Put the mascarpone in a medium-sized saucepan with the cream and the crushed peppercorns and bring just to the boil, stirring until smooth. Remove from the heat and then add the gelatine. Stir until dissolved (about 1 minute) then tip in the chocolate. Leave until melted.

3 Pour into a jug and then pour it into the moulds, stirring between each pour in order to distribute the peppercorns evenly. Chill for several hours or overnight until set.

4 Meanwhile, make the chocolate scribbles.

5 Blend the strawberries in a food processor with a little icing sugar and 1 tablespoon water until smooth. Test for sweetness, adding more sugar if necessary.

6 Loosen the edges of the moulds with a knife and shake them out on to serving plates. Spoon the sauce around and decorate with piped chocolate scribbles and some strawberries.

Iced banana and yogurt torte with pistachios and passion fruit

Preparation time **25 minutes**,
plus freezing

Serves **6**

1 medium ripe banana, about
175 g (6 oz), with skin on
300 g (10 oz) low-fat natural yogurt
200 g (7 oz) reduced-fat
mascarpone cheese
3 tablespoons granulated sweetener
2 passion fruit, halved
grated rind and juice of 1 lime
25 g (1 oz) pistachio nuts, roughly
chopped, plus extra to decorate
2 egg whites
2 passion fruit, to decorate
(optional)

1 Line a 1 kg (2 lb) loaf tin with clingfilm and chill in the freezer for 15 minutes.

2 Peel the banana and mash it with a fork. Mix it with the yogurt, mascarpone and sweetener until smooth. Scoop the seeds from the passion fruit into the yogurt mixture and stir in the lime rind and juice and the nuts.

3 Whisk the egg whites until stiff, moist peaks form, then fold into the yogurt mixture. Spoon into the prepared tin and level the top. Freeze for 4 hours or overnight until firm.

4 Before serving, leave the torte to stand at room temperature for 10–20 minutes to soften slightly. Invert on to a chopping board, peel away the clingfilm and use a hot knife to cut thick slices. Transfer to serving plates, decorate with pistachio nuts and spoonfuls of the extra passion fruit seeds, if liked.

Iced brûlée

Preparation time **30 minutes**,
  plus standing and freezing
Cooking time **10 minutes**
Serves **6**

1 vanilla pod
300 ml (½ pint) full-fat milk
6 egg yolks
75 g (3 oz) caster sugar
300 ml (½ pint) double cream

Caramel
250 g (8 oz) granulated sugar
250 ml (8 fl oz) water

1 Slit the vanilla pod lengthways and put it in a saucepan. Pour in the milk, bring it almost to the boil, remove from the heat and leave to stand for 15 minutes.

2 Line a baking sheet with foil and with a pencil draw 6 circles, using an upturned ramekin dish as a guide. Brush the foil with oil. Follow step 2 on page 39 to make the caramel, and pour a little into the centre of each circle, so that it spreads to the outer edge.

3 Holding the vanilla pod against the side of the saucepan, use the tip of a knife to scrape the black seeds into the milk. Discard the casing. Use a fork to mix the eggs and sugar together in a bowl, reheat the milk, then stir it into the yolk mixture. Return the custard to the pan and heat gently, stirring, until it coats the back of a spoon. Leave to cool.

4 Whip the cream until it forms soft peaks, then fold it into the custard. Pour into a shallow, nonstick loaf tin and freeze for 2 hours. Beat the ice cream with a fork, return it to the freezer for a further 2 hours, then beat it again.

5 Line 6 ramekins with clingfilm and spoon in the ice cream. Freeze for 2 hours or until solid.

6 Lift the ice creams out of the ramekins by pulling on the clingfilm. Peel off the clingfilm. Set the ice creams on plates, peel off the sugar discs from the foil and place on top of the ice creams.

White chocolate, vanilla and pistachio mousse

Preparation time **25 minutes**,
    plus chilling
Cooking time **5 minutes**
Serves **6**

50 g (2 oz) shelled pistachio nuts
200 g (7 oz) white chocolate,
    chopped
150 ml (¼ pint) double cream
1 teaspoon vanilla bean paste
150 ml (¼ pint) Greek yogurt
4 egg whites
icing sugar, for dusting

1 Put the nuts in a heatproof bowl, cover with boiling water and leave to stand for 1 minute. Drain well and rub between several layers of kitchen paper to remove the skins and reveal the more attractive green nut. Transfer the nuts to a food processor and chop finely.

2 Put the chocolate and 3 tablespoons of the cream in a medium heatproof bowl. Set over a pan of gently simmering water, making sure the bottom of the bowl doesn't come into contact with the water. Heat until melted, stirring gently once or twice until smooth.

3 Lightly whip the remaining cream with the vanilla bean paste until it forms soft peaks, then stir in the yogurt. In a separate bowl, beat the egg whites until just stiff.

4 Beat the cream mixture into the melted chocolate, then fold in the egg whites. Spoon half the mousse into 6 small glass dishes or cups. Reserve some of the nuts for decoration and sprinkle the rest over the mousse. Add the remaining mousse and decorate with the reserved nuts. Chill for at least 1 hour until lightly set and serve dusted with icing sugar.

Honeyed banana soufflés with fresh figs

Preparation time **30 minutes**,
  plus chilling
Cooking time **13–14 minutes**
Serves **6**

4 tablespoons water
4 teaspoons powdered gelatine
4 eggs, separated
3 tablespoons thick-set
  flower honey
2 bananas, about 400 g (13 oz) in
  total, weighed with skins on
2 tablespoons freshly squeezed
  lemon juice
250 g (8 oz) low-fat Greek yogurt

To decorate
50 g (2 oz) flaked almonds, toasted
  and roughly chopped (optional)
1 fresh fig, cut into 6 wedges

1 Attach soufflé collars to 6 individual 7.5-cm (3-inch) diameter x 4-cm (1½-inch) deep soufflé dishes so that the paper stands 4 cm (1½ inches) higher than the top of each dish.

2 Put the water in a small heatproof bowl or mug and sprinkle over the gelatine, making sure that the water absorbs all the powder. Set aside for 5 minutes, then stand the bowl in a small saucepan half-filled with boiling water and simmer for 3–4 minutes, stirring occasionally, until the gelatine dissolves to leave a clear liquid.

3 Put the egg yolks and honey in a large heatproof bowl, then stand the bowl over a saucepan of simmering water so that the base of the bowl is not touching the water. Whisk using a hand-held electric whisk for about 10 minutes until the eggs are very thick and pale, and the whisk leaves a trail when lifted above the mixture. Remove the bowl from the heat and continue whisking until cool.

4 Gradually fold in the dissolved gelatine, adding it in a thin, steady stream. Mash the bananas on a plate with the lemon juice, then fold into the egg yolk mixture with the yogurt.

5 Whisk the egg whites into stiff, moist-looking peaks. Fold a large spoonful into the mixture to loosen it, then gently fold in the remaining egg whites. Spoon the mixture into the prepared soufflé dishes so that it stands above the rim of the dishes. Chill for 4 hours or until set.

6 To serve, snip the string off the soufflé collars and gently peel away the paper. Press the toasted almonds, if using, around the sides of the soufflés with a knife and arrange the fig wedges on top, to decorate.

Iced vanilla parfait with cherry compote

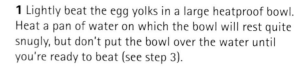

Preparation time **20 minutes**,
plus freezing
Cooking time **15 minutes**
Serves **6**

4 egg yolks
125 g (4 oz) granulated sugar
125 ml (4 fl oz) water
325 ml (11 fl oz) double cream
1½ teaspoons vanilla bean paste

Compote
400-g (14-oz can) stoned cherries
in syrup
1 teaspoon cornflour
3 tablespoons brandy

1 Lightly beat the egg yolks in a large heatproof bowl. Heat a pan of water on which the bowl will rest quite snugly, but don't put the bowl over the water until you're ready to beat (see step 3).

2 Put the sugar in a small, heavy-bottomed saucepan with the measured water and heat gently until the sugar dissolves. Bring the syrup to the boil and boil rapidly without stirring until it registers 115°C (239°F) on a sugar thermometer – soft ball stage.

3 Using a hand-held electric beater, slowly beat the sugar syrup into the egg yolks. Set the bowl over the pan of simmering water, making sure the bottom of the bowl doesn't come into contact with the water. Beat until the mixture is thick and foamy, then remove the bowl from the heat and beat until cool.

4 Lightly whip the cream with the vanilla bean paste and fold it into the beaten mixture. Turn the parfait into 6 small freezerproof serving dishes and freeze for at least 3 hours or overnight until firm.

5 Meanwhile, make the compote. Drain the cherries, reserving the syrup. Blend the cornflour with a little of the syrup in a small saucepan. Blend in the remaining syrup and cook over a moderate heat until thickened. Add the cherries and brandy and cook for a further minute. Turn the compote into a bowl and leave to cool. Serve with the parfait.

Hot desserts

Baked pear with almond crumble

Preparation time **10 minutes**
Cooking time **20 minutes**
Serves **4**

75 g (3 oz) wholemeal flour
65 g (2½ oz) ground almonds
75 g (3 oz) light brown sugar
65 g (2½ oz) butter
4 pears, unpeeled, quartered, cored
    and sliced lengthways
juice of 1 lime
2 tablespoons flaked almonds
150 g (5 oz) reduced-fat crème
    fraîche, to serve (optional)

1 Mix the flour, ground almonds and sugar together in a large bowl. Rub in the butter with your fingertips until it resembles fine breadcrumbs.

2 Arrange the pear slices in 4 tall, ovenproof ramekin dishes and drizzle with the lime juice.

3 Cover the pears with the crumble mixture and sprinkle over the flaked almonds.

4 Bake in a preheated oven, 220°C (425°F), Gas Mark 7, for 20 minutes and serve warm, topped with the crème fraîche, if liked.

Sweet soufflé omelette with strawberries

Preparation time **15 minutes**
Cooking time **8–10 minutes**
Serves **4**

375 g (12 oz) strawberries, hulled
    and thickly sliced, plus extra
    to decorate
2 tablespoons redcurrant jelly
2 teaspoons balsamic vinegar
5 eggs, separated
4 tablespoons icing sugar, sifted
25 g (1 oz) butter

1 Warm the sliced strawberries, redcurrant jelly and vinegar together in a saucepan until the jelly has just melted.

2 Meanwhile, whisk the egg whites into stiff, moist-looking peaks. Mix the egg yolks with 1 tablespoon of the sugar, then fold into the egg whites.

3 Heat the butter in a large frying pan, add the egg mixture and cook over a medium heat for 3–4 minutes until the underside is golden. Quickly transfer the pan to a hot grill and cook for 2–3 minutes until the top is browned and the centre still slightly soft, making sure that the handle is away from the heat.

4 Spoon the warm strawberry mixture over the omelette, fold in half and dust with the remaining sugar. Cut into 4 and serve straight away with a few extra strawberries.

Apple, blackberry and vanilla puffs

Preparation time **20 minutes**,
   plus cooling
Cooking time **25 minutes**
Makes **6**

3 cooking apples, about 550 g
   (1 lb 2 oz)
5 tablespoons caster sugar
2 tablespoons water
1½ teaspoons vanilla bean paste
½ teaspoon cornflour
150 g (5 oz) blackberries
500 g (1 lb) puff pastry, thawed
   if frozen
beaten egg, to glaze
vanilla sugar (see page 66),
   for dusting

Crème anglaise

1 vanilla pod
3 bay leaves or 3 rosemary sprigs
330 ml (11 fl oz) milk
330 ml (11 fl oz) single cream
6 egg yolks
2 tablespoons caster sugar

1 Peel and core the apples, then chop them into chunky pieces. Put the caster sugar in a medium saucepan with 2 tablespoons water and the vanilla bean paste. Heat gently until the sugar dissolves. Add the apples, turning them in the syrup, cover and simmer gently for 1 minute.

2 Blend the cornflour with 1 tablespoon water and add to the pan. Cook, stirring gently, until the juices thicken. Remove from the heat and transfer to a bowl to cool.

3 Grease a large baking sheet. Add the blackberries to the apple mixture and stir in. Thinly roll out the pastry on a lightly floured surface and cut 6 circles, 19 cm (7½ inches) across, using a bowl as a guide. Brush each edge with beaten egg and spoon the fruit mixture into the centre.

4 Fold one side of the pastry over to meet the other and press the edges together to seal. Transfer to the baking sheet. Brush the pastries with beaten egg and lightly score each one. Sprinkle with vanilla sugar and bake in a preheated oven, 200°C (400°F), Gas Mark 6, for 18–20 minutes or until they are risen and deep golden.

5 To make the crème anglaise, use a sharp knife to score the vanilla pod lengthways through to the centre. Put it in a heavy-based saucepan with the rosemary or bay leaves, milk and cream and bring slowly to the boil. Remove from the heat and leave to infuse for 20 minutes.

6 Beat the egg yolks and sugar in a bowl. Remove the herbs and vanilla pod from the milk, scrape out the vanilla seeds with the tip of a knife and return to the milk.

7 Pour the milk over the eggs and sugar, beating well. Return to a cleaned pan and cook over a gentle heat, stirring constantly with a wooden spoon until thick enough to coat the spoon. This may take 10 minutes. Pour into a jug and serve warm.

Italian rice pudding

Preparation time **10 minutes**,
  plus infusing
Cooking time **25 minutes**
Serves **3–4**

50 g (2 oz) raisins
3 tablespoons Marsala
1 vanilla pod
600 ml (1 pint) milk
2½ tablespoons caster sugar
finely grated rind of ½ orange, plus
  extra for decorating
¼ teaspoon ground cinnamon
100 g (3½ oz) risotto rice
125 ml (4 fl oz) double cream
toasted flaked almonds, to decorate

1 Put the raisins and Marsala in a bowl and leave to stand while you make the risotto. Use the tip of a small, sharp knife to score the vanilla pod lengthways through to the centre. Put it in a medium, heavy-bottomed saucepan with the milk, bring just to the boil, then remove from the heat and leave to infuse for 20 minutes.

2 Stir in the sugar, orange rind and cinnamon and return the pan to the heat. Tip in the rice and cook very gently, stirring frequently, for about 20 minutes until the mixture is thick and creamy and the rice is tender.

3 Stir in the steeped raisins and cream and heat gently for an additional 2 minutes. Serve warm, decorated with flaked almonds and grated orange rind.

Hot vanilla soufflés with apricot coulis

Preparation time **25 minutes**
Cooking time **25 minutes**
Serves **8**

75 g (3 oz) caster sugar, plus extra
for dusting
250 g (8 oz) no-soak dried apricots,
coarsely chopped
125 ml (4 fl oz) water
3 tablespoons cornflour
1 tablespoon water
5 tablespoons Cointreau or other
orange-flavoured liqueur
150 ml (¼ pint) milk
2 teaspoons vanilla bean paste
125 ml (4 fl oz) double cream
4 eggs, separated
icing sugar, for dusting

1 Grease 8 150-ml (¼-pint) ramekin dishes and dust each one lightly with caster sugar. Put the apricots in a small saucepan with the measured water and simmer gently for 3 minutes until softened. Blend ½ teaspoon of the cornflour with 1 tablespoon water and then add it to the pan. Cook gently for 1 minute or until the sauce has thickened. Turn it into a food processor or blender, add the liqueur, and blend until smooth. Divide the mixture between the ramekins.

2 Blend the remaining cornflour in a saucepan with a little of the milk. Add the remaining milk and heat gently, stirring, until thickened. Stir in 50 g (2 oz) of the caster sugar, the vanilla bean paste, cream and the egg yolks and pour into a large bowl.

3 Whisk the egg whites until stiff and gradually whisk in the remaining caster sugar. Using a large metal spoon, fold the egg whites into the custard.

4 Spoon the mixture into the ramekins and put them on a baking sheet. Bake in a preheated oven, 200°C (400°F), Gas Mark 6, for about 20 minutes until well risen. Dust with icing sugar and serve immediately.

Steamed pudding with syrupy mango topping

Preparation time **20 minutes**
Cooking time **1 hour 40 minutes**
Serves **6**

Vanilla syrup
(Make in advance)
175 g (6 oz) caster sugar
240 ml (8 fl oz)
2 vanilla pods

1 medium mango, halved
   and stoned
2 tablespoons vanilla syrup, plus
   extra for serving
125 g (4 oz) unsalted butter,
   softened
125 g (4 oz) caster sugar
1 teaspoon vanilla extract
2 eggs
175 g (6 oz) self-raising flour
4 tablespoons desiccated coconut
1 tablespoon milk

Crème anglais, to serve (see
   page 45)

1 To make the vanilla syrup, put the sugar into a small, heavy-bottom pan with half of the water and heat gently, stirring until the sugar dissolves. Bring to the boil and boil rapidly, without stirring, for 6–8 minutes until the syrup is deep golden. Dip the bottom of the pan into cold water to prevent further cooking. Stir in the remaining water.

2 Use a small, sharp knife to score each vanilla pod lengthways through to the centre. Add them to the syrup and return to the heat. Cook gently, stirring, until the caramel is smooth. Cool completely and transfer the syrup and vanilla pods to a clean bottle and stand for several days before use, shaking the bottle frequently.

3 To make the pudding on the day required, grease a 1.2-litre (2-pint) heatproof ovenproof bowl and line the bottom with a circle of greaseproof paper. Cut away the mango skin and cut the flesh into chunks. Scatter them in the prepared bowl and drizzle with the vanilla syrup.

4 Put the butter, sugar, vanilla extract, eggs and flour in a bowl and beat with a hand-held electric beater for 1–2 minutes until creamy. Stir in the coconut and milk and pour the mixture into the ovenproof bowl. Level the surface.

5 Cover the bowl with a double thickness of greaseproof paper and secure under the rim with string. Cover with foil, tucking the edges firmly under the rim.

6 Put the bowl in a steamer or large saucepan. Half-fill the pan with boiling water and cover with a tight-fitting lid. Steam gently for 1 hour 40 minutes, topping up the water as necessary, then leave to stand for 10 minutes.

7 Invert the pudding onto a serving plate and drizzle with extra vanilla syrup. Serve with crème anglaise (see page 45).

Sweet pancakes

Preparation time **5 minutes**,
   plus resting (optional)
Cooking time **15–25 minutes**
Makes **8–10 pancakes**

125 g (4 oz) plain flour
pinch of salt
2 tablespoons caster sugar
1 egg, lightly beaten
300 ml (½ pint) milk
25 g (1 oz) unsalted butter, melted
light olive oil, vegetable oil or
   butter, for greasing the pan

1 Put the flour, salt and sugar into a bowl and make a well in the centre. Pour the egg and a little of the milk into the well. Whisk the liquid, gradually incorporating the flour to make a smooth paste. Whisk in the butter, then the remaining milk until smooth. Pour the batter into a jug. Allow to rest, if liked.

2 Put a little oil or butter in an 18-cm (7-inch) pancake pan or heavy-based frying pan and heat until it starts to smoke. Pour off the excess and pour a little batter into the pan, tilting the pan until the base is coated in a thin layer. (If you prefer, use a small ladle to measure the batter into the pan.) Cook for 1–2 minutes until the underside is turning golden.

3 Flip the pancake with a palette knife and cook for a further 30–45 seconds until golden on the second side. Slide the pancake out of the pan and make the remaining pancakes, greasing the pan as necessary. Serve plain or filled with Glossy Chocolate Sauce (see page 57).

Crêpes suzette

Preparation time **10 minutes**,
    plus making the pancakes
Cooking time **10 minutes**
Serves **4**

125 g (4 oz) plain flour
pinch of salt
1 egg, lightly beaten
300 ml (½ pint) milk
light olive oil, vegetable oil or
    butter, for greasing the pan

Orange sauce
50 g (2 oz) butter
50 g (2 oz) caster sugar
grated rind and juice of 2 oranges
2 tablespoons Grand Marnier
2 tablespoons brandy

crème fraîche, to serve

1 To make the pancakes, put the flour and salt into a bowl and make a well in the centre. Pour the egg and a little of the milk into the well. Whisk the liquid, gradually incorporating the flour to make a smooth paste. Whisk in the remaining milk, then pour the batter into a jug. Allow to rest, if liked.

2 Put a little oil or butter into an 18-cm (7-inch) pancake pan or heavy-based frying pan and heat until it starts to smoke. Pour off the excess oil and pour a little batter into the pan, tilting the pan until the base is coated in a thin layer. (If you prefer, use a small ladle to measure the batter into the pan.) Cook the pancake for 1–2 minutes until the underside is turning golden.

3 Flip the pancake with a palette knife and cook for a further 30–45 seconds until it is golden on the second side. Slide the pancake out of the pan and make the remaining pancakes, oiling the pan as necessary. This quantity of batter will make 8–10 pancakes. Set the pancakes aside.

4 To make the sauce, melt the butter in a frying pan, add the sugar, orange rind and juice and heat until bubbling. Dip each pancake into the sauce, fold it into quarters and place on a warmed serving dish.

5 Add the Grand Marnier and brandy to the pan; heat gently, then ignite. Pour the flaming liquid over the pancakes and serve immediately with crème fraîche.

White chocolate brioche pudding

Preparation time **15 minutes**,
  plus soaking
Cooking time **30 minutes**
Serves **6**

butter, for greasing
250 g (8 oz) white chocolate,
  broken up
25 g (1 oz) unsalted butter
250 g (8 oz) brioche, sliced
250 g (8 oz) fresh or
  frozen raspberries
4 eggs
600 ml (1 pint) milk
25 g (1 oz) caster sugar
icing sugar, for dusting

1 Butter the sides of a shallow 2-litre (3½-pint) ovenproof dish. Melt the chocolate with the butter in a small bowl. If the brioche came from a large loaf, cut the slices into smaller triangles or squares. Lay half the bread slices in the dish and spoon over half the chocolate sauce. Scatter with half the raspberries.

2 Lay the rest of the bread over the top and dot with the remaining sauce and raspberries. Beat together the eggs, milk and sugar and pour the mixture over the pudding. Leave to soak for 20 minutes.

3 Bake in a preheated oven, 190°C (375°F), Gas Mark 5, for about 30 minutes until the surface is turning pale golden and the custard is very lightly set. Leave to stand for 10 minutes, then serve dusted with icing sugar.

Upside-down grapefruit sponge cakes

Preparation time **15 minutes**
Cooking time **40 minutes**
Serves **6**

1 grapefruit, peeled and cut into
   6 thin slices
6 tablespoons golden syrup
175 g (6 oz) unsalted butter, at
   room temperature
250 g (8 oz) demerara sugar
2 eggs
175 g (6 oz) self-raising flour
dash of salt
finely grated rind of 1 lime
2 tablespoons grapefruit juice
2–3 tablespoons milk

Crème anglais, to serve (see
   page 45)

1 Butter 6 individual pudding moulds or ramekins. Push a slice of grapefruit down on to the bottom of each, and drizzle with a tablespoon of golden syrup. Set aside.

2 Cream together the butter and sugar until light and fluffy. Add the eggs, one at a time, beating well until incorporated. Gently fold in the flour, salt and lime rind, using a metal spoon. Fold in the grapefruit juice and milk so that the mixture has a good dropping consistency.

3 Carefully spoon the mixture into the moulds and smooth down. Place the moulds in a large roasting tin, half-fill the tin with boiling water, and cook in a preheated oven, 180°C (350°F), Gas Mark 4, for about 40 minutes, or until risen and golden.

4 While the sponges are cooking, make the crème anglaise. Pour into a serving jug.

5 Remove the sponges from the oven, carefully lift out of the hot water and leave to cool in their moulds for 5 minutes. Loosen the sides of the sponges by running a knife around the inside of the moulds and then carefully turn out into serving bowls. Serve immediately with the crème anglaise.

Hot chocolate pancakes
with spiced ricotta and raisins

Preparation time **20 minutes**, plus
   making pancakes and sauce
Cooking time **about 10 minutes**
Serves **4**

Chocolate pancakes

100 g (3½ oz) plain flour
15 g (½ oz) cocoa powder
2 tablespoons caster sugar
1 egg
300 ml (½ pint) milk
vegetable oil or butter, for frying

Filling

1 piece of stem ginger, about
   15 g (½ oz), finely chopped
2 tablespoons caster sugar, plus
   extra for dusting
250 g (8 oz) ricotta cheese
50 g (2 oz) raisins
150 g (5 oz) white chocolate,
   finely chopped
3 tablespoons double cream

Glossy chocolate sauce

125 g (4 oz) caster sugar
100 ml (3½ fl oz) water
200 g (7 oz) plain dark chocolate,
   broken into pieces
25 g (1 oz) unsalted butter, plus
   extra for greasing

lightly whipped cream, to serve
   (optional)

1 To make the pancakes, sift the flour and cocoa powder into a bowl, then stir in the sugar. Add the egg and a little milk, and whisk to make a stiff batter. Beat in the remaining milk.

2 Put a little oil or butter in an 18-cm (7-inch) pancake pan or heavy-based frying pan and heat until it starts to smoke. Pour off the excess and pour a little batter into the pan, tilting it until the base is coated in a thin layer. (Or, if you prefer, use a small ladle to measure the batter into the pan.) Cook for 1–2 minutes until the underside begins to turn golden.

3 Flip the pancake with a palette knife and cook for a further 30–45 seconds on the second side. Slide the pancake out of the pan and make the remaining pancakes, greasing the pan as necessary. (This quantity of batter will make about 8 pancakes.) Set the pancakes aside while making the filling.

4 To make the filling, mix the ginger in a bowl with the sugar, ricotta, raisins, white chocolate and cream. Place spoonfuls of the filling in the centres of the pancakes and fold them into quarters, enclosing the filling.

5 Place the pancakes in a lightly greased, shallow ovenproof dish and dust with sugar. Bake in a preheated oven, 200°C (400°F), Gas Mark 6, for 10 minutes until heated through.

6 Meanwhile, make the sauce. Heat the caster sugar and water in a small heavy-based saucepan until the sugar has dissolved. Bring the syrup to the boil and boil rapidly for 1 minute. Remove the pan from the heat and add the chocolate. Leave until melted, then stir in the butter to make a smooth glossy sauce. Serve hot, with the pancakes.

Sunken torte with orange liqueur cream

Preparation time **20 minutes**
Cooking time **30 minutes**
Serves **8**

250 g (8 oz) plain dark chocolate,
   broken up
125 g (4 oz) unsalted butter
1 teaspoon vanilla extract
6 medium eggs, separated
125 g (4 oz) light muscovado sugar

Orange liqueur cream
250 ml (8 fl oz) Greek yogurt
finely grated rind and juice
   of ½ orange
2 tablespoons orange liqueur
2 tablespoons icing sugar

chocolate curls, to decorate (see
   page 10)

1 Grease and line a 23-cm (9-inch) springform or loose-bottomed cake tin with greaseproof paper, then grease the paper. Melt the chocolate with the butter in a small bowl and stir in the vanilla extract.

2 Whisk the egg yolks with 100 g (3½ oz) of the sugar in a large bowl for 3–4 minutes until the mixture leaves a trail when the whisk is lifted from the bowl. Fold in the chocolate mixture.

3 Whisk the egg whites in a clean bowl until peaking. Gradually whisk in the remaining sugar. Fold a quarter of the whisked whites into the chocolate mixture to lighten it, then fold in the remainder.

4 Turn into the tin and bake in a preheated oven, 160°C (325°F), Gas Mark 3, for 30 minutes or until well risen and springy. (This chocolate cake rises during baking only to sink again as it cools. Don't be put off: the moist density of the mixture makes it utterly delicious.)

5 Beat together the yogurt, orange rind and juice, liqueur and icing sugar until smooth, then chill. Cool the cake in the tin for 10 minutes before serving with the orange cream and chocolate curls.

Hot chocolate and Kahlua risotto

Preparation time **10 minutes**
Cooking time **15 minutes**
Serves **4**

450 ml (¾ pint) milk
15 g (½ oz) caster sugar
125 g (4 oz) risotto rice
4 tablespoons Kahlua or other
    coffee liqueur
150 g (5 oz) plain dark chocolate,
    roughly chopped
15 g (½ oz) chocolate coffee
    beans, crushed
crème fraîche, to serve

1 Put the milk in a large heavy-based saucepan with the sugar and heat until it is almost beginning to boil. Sprinkle in the rice, stirring, then reduce the heat to a very gentle simmer.

2 Cook the risotto gently for about 15 minutes, stirring frequently, until it is creamy and the rice has softened but still retains a nutty texture. (If the risotto becomes dry before the rice is cooked, add a splash more milk.)

3 Stir in the liqueur and half the chocolate and stir until the chocolate has melted. Quickly stir in the remaining chocolate and ladle into small, warmed bowls or coffee cups. Scatter with the coffee beans and serve with crème fraîche for swirling into the risotto.

Sticky toffee puddings

Preparation time **20 minutes**
Cooking time **45–50 minutes**
Serves **8**

125 g (4 oz) stoned dates, chopped
150 ml (5 fl oz) water
125 g (4 oz) unsalted butter,
    softened
125 g (4 oz) caster sugar
2 teaspoons vanilla bean paste
3 eggs
175 g (6 oz) self-raising flour
1 teaspoon baking powder
cream or ice cream, to serve

Sauce

300 ml (½ pint) double cream
175 g (6 oz) light muscovado sugar
50 g (2 oz) butter

1 Put the dates in a small saucepan with the measured water and bring to the boil. Simmer gently for 5 minutes until the dates are soft and pulpy. Blend to a purée using a hand-held blender or transfer them to a food processor and blend. Leave to cool.

2 Meanwhile, make the sauce. Put half the cream in a small, heavy-bottomed saucepan with the muscovado sugar and butter and heat until the sugar dissolves. Bring to the boil, then let the sauce bubble for about 5 minutes until it turns to a rich, dark caramel. Stir in the remaining cream and reserve.

3 Grease 8 metal 150-ml (¼-pint) pudding moulds and line the bottoms with circles of greaseproof paper. Put the unsalted butter, caster sugar, vanilla bean paste, eggs, flour and baking powder in a bowl and beat with a hand-held electric beater for 1–2 minutes until pale and creamy.

4 Stir the date purée into the pudding mixture and divide it between the pudding moulds. Level the tops and place the moulds in a roasting tin. Pour boiling water to a depth of 1.5 cm (¾ inch) into the tin and cover with foil. Bake the puddings in a preheated oven, 180°C (350°F), Gas Mark 4, for 35–40 minutes or until they are risen and feel firm to the touch.

5 Leave the puddings in the moulds while you reheat the toffee sauce, then loosen the edges of the moulds and invert the puddings onto serving plates. Cover with plenty of the sauce and serve with additional cream or ice cream.

Chocolate fudge fondue

Preparation time **15 minutes**
Cooking time **10 minutes**
Serves **6**

150 g (5 oz) light muscovado sugar
100 ml (3½ fl oz) water
50 g (2 oz) unsalted butter
200 g (7 oz) plain dark chocolate,
    chopped
1 teaspoon vanilla extract
100 ml (3½ fl oz) soured cream
2 bananas
200 g (7 oz) sweet raisin bread
handful of strawberries and cherries

1 Put the sugar in a small heavy-based saucepan with the measured water. Heat gently until the sugar has dissolved, then bring to the boil and boil rapidly for about 4 minutes until the syrup is bubbling vigorously and looks dark and treacly.

2 Remove the saucepan from the heat and immerse the base in cold water to prevent further cooking. Add 2 tablespoons water, taking care because the syrup is likely to splutter. Return the saucepan to the heat and cook, stirring, until the syrup is smooth and glossy.

3 Add the butter, chocolate and vanilla extract and leave until melted, stirring frequently until the mixture is completely smooth. Stir in the cream and leave to stand while you prepare the dippers.

4 Cut the bananas diagonally into chunky pieces. Cut the bread into small, bite-sized chunks. Reheat the sauce until it is warm but not piping hot and pour into small serving cups. Arrange the fruit and bread around the cups to serve.

Tarts and pies

Portuguese custard tarts

Preparation time **25 minutes**
Cooking time **40 minutes**
Makes **12**

1 tablespoon vanilla sugar
    (see below)
½ teaspoon ground cinnamon
500 g (1 lb) sweet shortcrust pastry,
    thawed if frozen
3 eggs
2 egg yolks
2 tablespoons caster sugar
1 teaspoon vanilla bean paste
325 ml (11 fl oz) double cream
150 ml (¼ pint) milk
icing sugar, for dusting

Vanilla sugar
2 vanilla pods
225 g (8 oz) caster sugar

1 To make the vanilla sugar, use a small, sharp knife to cut each vanilla pod in half lengthways, then cut each length in half to make 8 pieces. Put the sugar in a glass jar and push the vanilla pieces into it. Cover with a lid and store for about a week before using, shaking the jar occasionally to disperse the vanilla flavour. The sugar will keep for several weeks.

2 Mix the vanilla sugar with the cinnamon. Cut the pastry in half and roll out each piece to a 20 x 20-cm (8 x 8-inch) square. Sprinkle one square with the spiced sugar and position the second square on top. Re-roll the pastry to a 40 x 30-cm (16 x 12-inch) rectangle and cut out 12 circles, each 10 cm (4 inches) across, using a large cutter or small bowl as a guide.

3 Pack the pastry circles into the sections of a nonstick deep bun tin, pressing them firmly into the bottom and around the sides. Line each one with a square of foil and bake blind in a preheated oven, 200°C (400°F), Gas Mark 6, for 15 minutes. Remove the foil and bake for a further 5 minutes. Reduce the oven temperature to 170°C (325°F), Gas Mark 3.

4 Beat together the eggs, egg yolks, caster sugar and vanilla bean paste. Heat the cream and milk in a saucepan until it is bubbling around the edges and pour it over the egg mixture, stirring. Strain the custard into a jug and pour carefully into the pastry cases. Bake for about 20 minutes or until the custard is only just set. Leave the tarts to cool in the tin and serve dusted with icing sugar.

Tarte tatin

Preparation time **20 minutes**,
   plus chilling
Cooking time **35–40 minutes**
Serves **4–6**

1 quantity pâte sucrée (see
   page 78)
50 g (2 oz) unsalted butter
50 g (2 oz) caster sugar
6 dessert apples, such as Cox,
   peeled, cored and quartered
thick cream or crème fraîche,
   to serve (optional)

1 Make the pastry (see page 78). Wrap it closely in clingfilm and leave it to chill for 30 minutes.

2 Melt the butter and sugar in a 20-cm (8-inch) ovenproof frying pan. When the mixture is golden brown, add the apples and toss them in the syrup to coat them. Cook for a few minutes until the apples start to caramelize.

3 Roll out the pastry on a lightly floured surface to a round, a little larger than the pan. Put it over the apples, tucking the edges of the pastry inside the edge of the pan until it fits neatly.

4 Bake in a preheated oven, 200°C (400°F), Gas Mark 6, for 35–40 minutes until the pastry is golden. Leave to cool in the pan for 5 minutes, then put a large plate on top of the pan and invert the tart on to it. Serve warm with thick cream or crème fraîche, if liked.

Treacle tart

Preparation time **20 minutes**,
plus chilling
Cooking time **30–35 minutes**
Serves **6**

275 g (9 oz) golden syrup
175 g (6 oz) fresh white
    breadcrumbs
grated rind and juice of 2 lemons

Shortcrust pastry
200 g (7 oz) plain flour
pinch of salt
100 g (3½ oz) fat, such as equal
    quantities of butter and white
    vegetable fat
2–3 tablespoons iced water

1 To make the pastry, sift the flour and salt into a bowl. Cut the fat into small pieces and add it to the flour. Use your fingertips to rub the fat into the flour very lightly and evenly until it begins to resemble fine breadcrumbs. Sprinkle the water over the surface and stir with a palette knife until the mixture begins to clump together.

2 Turn out the pastry on to a lightly floured surface and press it together lightly with the fingers. Chill for about 30 minutes before use.

3 Roll the pastry out and line a deep 20-cm (8-inch) tart tin. Trim the edges.

4 Warm the golden syrup in a saucepan until it is runny, then remove the pan from the heat and stir in the breadcrumbs, lemon rind and juice. Spread the mixture over the pastry case.

5 Bake the tart in a preheated oven, 190°C (375°F), Gas Mark 5, for 30–35 minutes until the pastry is crisp and golden. Serve warm or cold, drizzled with golden syrup.

Chocolate fig tatin

Preparation time **20 minutes**
Cooking time **35 minutes**
Serves **6**

100 g (3½ oz) plain dark chocolate,
   grated
1 teaspoon ground mixed spice
75 g (3 oz) caster sugar, plus
   2 tablespoons
500 g (1 lb) puff pastry, thawed
   if frozen
75 g (3 oz) unsalted butter, plus
   extra for greasing
10 fresh figs, quartered
1 tablespoon lemon juice
vanilla ice cream or crème fraîche,
   to serve

1 Mix together the grated chocolate, spice and
2 tablespoons sugar. Cut the pastry into 3 evenly sized
pieces and roll out each to a circle 25 cm (10 inches)
across, using a plate or inverted bowl as a guide.

2 Scatter 2 rounds to within 1.5 cm (¾ inch) of the
edges with the grated chocolate mixture. Stack the
pastry layers so that the chocolate is sandwiched in
2 layers. Press the pastry down firmly around the edges.

3 Lightly butter the sides of a shallow 23-cm (9-inch)
round baking tin, 3.5 cm (1½ inches) deep. (Don't use a
loose-bottomed tin.) Melt the butter in a frying pan. Add
the sugar and heat gently until dissolved. Add the figs
and cook for 3 minutes or until lightly coloured and the
syrup begins to turn golden. Add the lemon juice.

4 Tip the figs into the tin, spreading them evenly. Lay
the pastry over them, tucking the dough down inside the
tin edges. Bake in a preheated oven, 200°C (400°F), Gas
Mark 6, for 30 minutes until risen and golden. Leave for
5 minutes, loosen the edges and invert on to a plate.

Blueberry pie

Preparation time **25 minutes**,
    plus chilling
Cooking time **30–35 minutes**
Serves 6

2 quantities pâte sucrée
    (see page 78)
250 g (8 oz) fresh or frozen
    blueberries, thawed if frozen
25 g (1 oz) sugar
milk, to glaze
50 g (2 oz) flaked almonds,
    to decorate
cream or crème fraîche, to serve
    (optional)

1 Make the pastry (see page 78). Roll out about two-thirds of it and line a 23-cm (9-inch) tart tin. Chill for 30 minutes. Spread the blueberries evenly over the pastry case and sprinkle with the sugar.

2 Roll out the remaining pastry and cut into thin strips. Brush the rim of the tart with water and arrange the pastry strips in a lattice pattern over the top.

3 Brush the pastry with a little milk and sprinkle the flaked almonds over the surface.

4 Bake in a preheated oven, 190°C (375°F), Gas Mark 5, for 30–35 minutes until the pastry is golden and the blueberries are tender. Serve warm or cold with cream or crème fraîche, if liked.

Lemon meringue pie

Preparation time **35 minutes**,
plus chilling
Cooking time **50 minutes**
Serves **6**

1 quantity pâte sucrée (see
page 78)
25 g (1 oz) cornflour
100 g (3½ oz) caster sugar
150 ml (¼ pint) water
grated rind of 2 lemons
juice of 1 lemon
25 g (1 oz) butter
2 egg yolks

Meringue
3 egg whites
175 g (6 oz) caster sugar

1 Make the pastry (see page 78). Roll it out and line a
20 cm (8 inch) tart tin. Chill for 30 minutes, then bake
blind in a preheated oven, 200°C (400°F), Gas Mark 6,
for 15 minutes. Remove the paper and beans or foil and
return to the oven for a further 5 minutes.

2 Mix the cornflour and caster sugar in a saucepan. Stir
in the water, lemon rind and juice until well blended.
Bring to the boil, stirring until the sauce is thickened
and smooth. Take it off the heat and stir in the butter.
Leave to cool slightly.

3 Whisk the egg yolks in a bowl. Whisk in 2 tablespoons
of the sauce and return this mixture to the pan. Cook
gently until the sauce has thickened further and pour it
into the pastry case. Return to the oven for 15 minutes
until the filling has set.

4 Whisk the egg whites until stiff and dry. Whisk in
1 tablespoon of sugar, then fold in the rest. Spread it to
cover all of the filling. Return to the oven for 10 minutes
until the meringue is golden. Serve warm or cold.

Chocolate, rosemary and pine nut tart

Preparation time **20 minutes**,
  plus chilling
Cooking time **45 minutes**
Serves **10–12**

375 g (12 oz) white chocolate
50 g (2 oz) unsalted butter
50 g (2 oz) caster sugar
3 eggs
1 tablespoon finely chopped
  rosemary
finely grated rind and juice of
  1 lemon
125 g (4 oz) self-raising flour
75 g (3 oz) pine nuts
icing sugar, for dusting

Crisp chocolate pastry
15 g (½ oz) cocoa powder
125 g (4 oz) plain flour
25 g (1 oz) icing sugar
75 g (3 oz) lightly salted
  butter, diced
1 egg yolk
1 teaspoon cold water

1 To make the pastry, sift the cocoa powder, flour and icing sugar into a bowl. Add the butter and then rub in with the fingertips until the mixture resembles fine breadcrumbs. Add the egg yolk and 1 teaspoon cold water and mix to a dough. Alternatively, blend the butter into the flour mixture in a food processor, then blend in the egg yolk and water until the mixture binds together.

2 Turn the dough on to a lightly floured surface and knead lightly until smooth. Wrap and chill for at least 30 minutes before using.

3 Thinly roll out the pastry on a lightly floured surface and use it to line a 25-cm (10-inch) loose-bottomed flan tin, 2.5 cm (1 inch) deep. Line with greaseproof paper and baking beans and bake blind in a preheated oven, 200°C (400°F), Gas Mark 6, for 15 minutes. Remove the paper and beans and bake for a further 5 minutes. Reduce the oven temperature to 160°C (325°F), Gas Mark 3.

4 Chop 250 g (8 oz) of the chocolate. Break the remainder into pieces and melt it with the butter. Whisk together the sugar, eggs and rosemary in a large bowl. Stir in the melted chocolate mixture, lemon rind and juice and flour. Gently stir in all but 50 g (2 oz) of the chopped chocolate.

5 Turn the mixture into the pastry case. Scatter the pine nuts and remaining chocolate over the top. Bake for about 25 minutes until pale golden and just firm. Serve warm, dusted with icing sugar.

Bakewell slice

Preparation time **20 minutes**
Cooking time **25 minutes**
Makes **12 pieces**

75 g (3 oz) polenta
75 g (3 oz) brown rice flour
½ teaspoon xanthan gum
grated rind of 1 lemon
100 g (3½ oz) butter, cubed
1 tablespoon golden caster sugar
1 egg yolk, beaten
4 tablespoons raspberry jam

Sponge
2 eggs
125 g (4 oz) caster sugar
125 g (4 oz) rice flour
125 g (4 oz) butter
50 g (2 oz) ground almonds
1 teaspoon gluten-free
    baking powder
50 g (2 oz) flaked almonds

1 Place the polenta, flour, xanthan gum, lemon rind, butter and sugar in a food processor and whizz until the mixture resembles fine breadcrumbs, or rub in by hand in a large bowl. Add the egg yolk and gently mix in using a knife, adding a little cold water if the mixture is too dry.

2 Place the pastry in a 28 x 18-cm (11 x 7-inch) deep baking tin and press it out to line the tin. Spread the jam over the pastry.

3 Place all the sponge ingredients except the flaked almonds in a food processor and whizz until smooth, or beat in a large bowl. Spoon the mixture into the baking tray, and place in a preheated oven, 200°C (400°F), Gas Mark 6, for 20–25 minutes until just firm and risen. Remove the tart from the oven and leave to cool.

4 Toast the flaked almonds for a few minutes under a grill until brown and scatter them over the top. Cut into 12 pieces.

Perfect pecan pies

Preparation time **15 minutes**,
    plus chilling
Cooking time **20 minutes**
Serves **8**

75 g (3 oz) brown rice flour, plus a
    little extra for dusting
50 g (2 oz) chickpea/gram flour
75 g (3 oz) polenta
1 teaspoon xanthan gum
125 g (4 oz) butter, cubed
2 tablespoons caster sugar
1 egg, beaten

Filling
100 g (3½ oz) light muscovado
    sugar
150 g (5 oz) butter
125 g (4 oz) honey
175 g (6 oz) pecan halves, half of
    them roughly chopped
2 eggs, beaten

1 Place the flours, polenta, xanthan gum and butter in a food processor and whizz to fine breadcrumbs, or rub in by hand in a large bowl. Stir in the sugar. Add the egg and gently mix in using a knife, adding enough cold water (probably a couple of teaspoons) to make a dough. Don't let it become too wet. Knead for a couple of minutes, wrap closely in clingfilm and chill for an hour.

2 Meanwhile, place the sugar, butter and honey for the filling in a medium saucepan and heat until the sugar has dissolved. Leave to cool for 10 minutes.

3 While the filling cools, knead the dough on a lightly dusted surface to soften it. Divide it into 8, then roll each piece out to a thickness of 2.5 mm (⅛ inch). Use to line 8 individual 11.5-cm (4½-inch) pie tins, rolling the rolling pin over the top to cut off the excess dough.

4 Stir the chopped pecans and eggs into the filling mixture and pour into the pastry-lined tins. Arrange the pecan halves on top, then place the tins in a preheated oven, 200°C (400°F), Gas Mark 6, for 15–20 minutes until the filling is firm. Remove and leave to cool.

French apple flan

Preparation time **30 minutes**,
   plus chilling
Cooking time **40–45 minutes**
Serves **8**

750 g (1½ lb) dessert apples
3 tablespoons lemon juice
4 tablespoons warmed, sieved
   apricot jam
175 ml (6 fl oz) single cream
2 eggs, beaten
50 g (2 oz) caster sugar

Pâte sucrée
175 g (6 oz) plain flour
pinch of salt
75 g (3 oz) unsalted butter,
   slightly softened
2 egg yolks
1 tablespoon cold water
40 g (1½ oz) caster sugar

icing sugar, for dusting

1 To make the pastry, sift the flour and salt into a pile on a cold surface and make a centre well. Add the butter, egg yolks, measured water and sugar to the well and use the fingertips of one hand to work together into a mixture that resembles scrambled egg. Work in the flour gradually with your fingertips to bind the mixture into a smooth dough. Press together lightly and form into a ball. Wrap in clingfilm and chill for 30 minutes.

2 Roll the pastry out and line a 25-cm (10-inch) tart tin. Chill the pastry case for 30 minutes.

3 Peel and core the apples. Slice them thinly into a bowl and toss with the lemon juice. Drain the apples and arrange them in concentric circles over the base of the pastry case.

4 Brush the apricot jam over the apple slices and bake the tart in a preheated oven, 220°C (425°F), Gas Mark 7, for 10 minutes.

5 Whisk the cream, eggs and sugar in a bowl. Pour the mixture carefully over the apples. Return to the preheated oven and bake at 190°C (375°F), Gas Mark 5, for 30–35 minutes until the pastry is golden and the filling is cooked. Sprinkle with icing sugar and serve warm.

Cranberry and apple tart with walnut crust

Preparation time **25 minutes**
Cooking time **1 hour 20 minutes**
Serves **6–8**

Crust
30 g (1¼ oz) walnut halves,
   finely chopped
175 g (6 oz) butter
75 g (3 oz) caster sugar
250 g (8 oz) plain flour

Sponge filling
125 g (4 oz) butter
125 g (4 oz) caster sugar
2 eggs, beaten
50 g (2 oz) self-raising flour
2 tablespoons cranberry jelly
   or sauce
1 cooking apple, peeled, cored
   and sliced
50 g (2 oz) fresh cranberries

1 Preheat the oven to 200°C (400°F), Gas Mark 6. Grease a 25-cm (10-inch) tin. To make the crust, put the walnuts, butter, sugar and flour in a food processor or bowl and mix, then add enough cold water to form a soft dough. Spoon into the tin and, using the back of a spoon, press over the base and up the sides. Bake for 30 minutes, or until golden brown.

2 To make the filling, beat together the butter and sugar until soft and fluffy. Add the eggs and flour, and beat until smooth.

3 Spread the cranberry jelly or sauce over the bottom of the cooked crust, then pour the filling over and smooth the top. Scatter the apple and cranberries over the sponge mixture.

4 Reduce the oven temperature to 190°C (375°F), Gas Mark 5. Bake the tart on the middle shelf of the oven for 40–50 minutes or until the filling is well risen and golden brown, and the centre is firm when pressed.

Classic pumpkin pie

Preparation time **30 minutes**,
  plus chilling time
Cooking time **50 minutes**
Serves **6–8**

250 g (8 oz) plain flour
150 g (5 oz) unsalted butter, cut
  into small pieces
3 tablespoons caster sugar
1–2 tablespoons cold water

Filling
1 pumpkin, about 750 g (1½ lb)
250 ml (8 fl oz) single cream
2 eggs
150 ml (4 fl oz) maple syrup
4 tablespoons plain flour
1 teaspoon ground ginger
1 teaspoon ground cinnamon

lightly whipped and sweetened
  cream, to serve

1 To make the pastry, put the flour into a food processor or blender, add the butter, and process until the mixture resembles breadcrumbs. Add the sugar and measured water and blend to a dough, adding a drop more water if the mixture is too crumbly. (Alternatively, sift the flour into a mixing bowl, rub in the butter, then add the sugar and water and mix to a dough.) Wrap the dough in foil and chill for 30 minutes.

2 Scoop out the seeds and fibres from the pumpkin. Cut the pumpkin into large wedges and cook in a steamer over a pan of gently simmering water for 15–20 minutes until the flesh is tender. Scoop the flesh away from the skin with a spoon and put it into a food processor or blender. Blend until smooth, then transfer to a bowl. Add the cream, eggs, maple syrup, flour and spices and beat until evenly combined.

3 Roll out the pastry on a lightly floured surface and use to line a 23-cm (9-inch) flan tin with a removable bottom, or a deep pie plate.

4 Pour the pumpkin mixture into the pastry case and place it on a baking sheet. Bake in a preheated oven at 200°C (400°F), Gas Mark 6, for about 30 minutes, until the pastry is golden and the filling feels just firm to the touch. Serve warm with lightly whipped and sweetened cream.

Key lime pie

Preparation time **30 minutes**,
  plus chilling
Cooking time **15–20 minutes**
Serves **8**

Base
150 g (5 oz) digestive
  biscuits, crushed
2 tablespoons caster sugar
75 g (3 oz) butter, melted

Filling
3 eggs, separated
400 g (13 oz) can sweetened
  condensed milk
125 ml (4 fl oz) freshly squeezed
  lime juice
1 tablespoon lemon juice
2 teaspoons grated lime rind
2 tablespoons caster sugar

Topping
250 ml (8 fl oz) double cream
1 tablespoon icing sugar
few drops of vanilla extract

lime slices, to decorate (optional)

1 Mix together the biscuit crumbs, sugar and melted butter and press over the bottom and up the sides of a 23-cm (9-inch) springform tin. Refrigerate while making the filling.

2 Lightly beat the egg yolks together until creamy. Add the condensed milk, lime and lemon juices and lime rind and beat until well mixed and slightly thickened.

3 In another bowl, beat the egg whites until frothy. Add the sugar and continue beating until the meringue holds soft peaks. Fold gently but thoroughly into the lime mixture using a large metal spoon.

4 Preheat the oven to 160°C (325°F), Gas Mark 3. Spoon the filling into the crumb crust and smooth the top. Bake in the oven for 15–20 minutes or until the filling is just firm and lightly browned on top. When cool, refrigerate the pie for at least 3 hours, until it is well chilled.

5 To make the topping, whip the cream until it begins to thicken. Add the sugar and vanilla extract and continue whipping until quite thick but not stiff. Spread the cream over the top of the chilled pie. Decorate with twisted lime slices, if liked. Remove the side of the tin just before serving, and serve well chilled, decorated with lime slices, if liked.

Classic lemon tart

Preparation time **20 minutes**,
  plus chilling
Cooking time **40–45 minutes**
Serves **8**

200 g (7 oz) plain flour
½ teaspoon salt
100 g (3½ oz) chilled butter, diced
2 tablespoons icing sugar, plus extra
  for dusting
2 egg yolks
1–2 teaspoons cold water

Filling
3 eggs, plus 1 egg yolk
475 ml (16 fl oz) double cream
125 g (4 oz) sugar
150 ml (¼ pint) lemon juice

1 Put the flour in a bowl, add the salt and diced butter, and rub in with the fingertips until the mixture resembles fine breadcrumbs. Stir in the sugar and gradually work in the egg yolks and measured water to make a firm dough.

2 Knead the dough briefly on a lightly floured surface, then cover with clingfilm and chill for 30 minutes. Roll out the dough and use to line a 25-cm (10-inch) fluted pie dish or flan tin. Prick the pastry case with a fork and chill for 20 minutes.

3 Line the pastry case with baking parchment and ceramic baking beans and cook in a preheated oven, 200°C (400°F), Gas Mark 6, for 10 minutes. Remove the paper and beans and bake for a further 10 minutes until crisp and golden. Remove from the oven and reduce the temperature to 150°C (300°F), Gas Mark 2.

4 Beat together all the filling ingredients, pour them into the pastry case and bake for 20–25 minutes, or until the filling is just set. Leave the tart to cool completely, dust with icing sugar and serve.

Double chocolate soufflé tart

Preparation time **40 minutes**,
  plus chilling
Cooking time **35 minutes**
Serves **6**

Pastry
200 g (7 oz) plain flour
2 tablespoons cocoa powder
50 g (2 oz) caster sugar
125 g (4 oz) butter, diced, plus extra
  for greasing
2½–3 tablespoons water

Filling
125 g (4 oz) white chocolate,
  broken into pieces
25 g (1 oz) butter
4 eggs, separated
75 g (3 oz) caster sugar
grated rind of ½ orange
75 g (3 oz) plain dark
  chocolate, chopped

To decorate
icing sugar, for dusting
white chocolate curls (see page 10)
orange rind swirls (see page 10)
orange segments, to serve

1 To make the tart case, put the flour, cocoa powder and caster sugar in a bowl and rub in the butter until fine crumbs are formed. Stir in enough water to make a soft, smooth dough. Knead lightly, roll out on a floured surface and line a 23-cm (9-inch) buttered, loose-bottomed tin. Trim excess pastry, prick the base and chill for 15 minutes.

2 Line the case with baking paper and baking beans. Set on a baking sheet and bake in a preheated oven, 190°C (375°F), Gas Mark 5, for 10 minutes. Remove the paper and beans and cook for 5 more minutes.

3 Reduce the oven temperature to 180°C (350°F), Gas Mark 4. Melt the white chocolate and butter in a large heatproof bowl set over a saucepan of just-boiled water.

4 Make the filling by whisking the egg yolks, caster sugar and orange rind in a large bowl until thick and pale. Fold in the melted white chocolate and butter.

5 Wash the whisk and dry it well, then use it to whisk the egg whites into stiff, moist-looking peaks. Fold a large spoonful into the white chocolate mixture to loosen it, then fold in the remaining egg whites.

6 Sprinkle the dark chocolate on to the base of the tart case, then cover with the white chocolate mixture. Bake for 20 minutes until the filling is well risen, the top feels crusty and there is a slight wobble to the centre. Leave to cool – as the tart cools, the filling will sink slightly.

7 Make the chocolate curls and orange rind swirls.

8 Remove the tart from the tin and place on a serving plate. Dust with icing sugar and top with the chocolate curls and orange rind swirls. Serve cut into wedges with some orange segments.

Macadamia and vanilla tart

Preparation time **30 minutes**
Cooking time **45 minutes**
Serves **8–10**

1 quantity sweet vanilla pastry
   (see below)
150 g (5 oz) macadamia nuts
100 g (3½ oz) light
   muscovado sugar
150 ml (¼ pint) maple syrup
75 g (3 oz) unsalted butter
2 teaspoons vanilla bean paste
150 g (5 oz) ground almonds
4 eggs, beaten

Sweet vanilla pastry
125 g (4 oz) plain flour
75 g (3 oz) lightly salted butter,
   diced
2 tablespoons Vanilla Sugar
   (see page 66)
1 egg yolk
2–3 teaspoons cold water

ice cream or cream, to serve

1 To make the pastry, put the flour in a bowl with the butter and cut in with the fingertips until the mixture resembles fine breadcrumbs. Stir in the sugar. Add the egg yolk and 2–3 teaspoons cold water and mix to a firm dough, adding a little more water if the dough feels dry. (Alternatively, blend the butter into the flour in a food processor, then blend in the sugar, egg yolk and water until the mixture binds together.) Chill the pastry.

2 Thinly roll out the pastry on a lightly floured work surface and use it to line a 23-cm (9-inch) loose-bottomed flan tin. Line the pastry with greaseproof paper and ceramic baking beans and bake blind in a preheated oven, 200°C (400°F), Gas Mark 6, for 15 minutes. Remove the paper and beans and bake for a further 5 minutes. Reduce the oven temperature to 180°C (325°F), Gas Mark 3.

3 Coarsely chop the macadamia nuts. Put the sugar, maple syrup and butter in a saucepan and heat gently until melted. Remove the pan from the heat and beat in the vanilla bean paste and ground almonds, followed by the eggs. Add half the nuts and pour the mixture into the pastry case.

4 Sprinkle the tart with the remaining nuts and bake for about 25 minutes or until the filling forms a crust but remains quite soft underneath. Leave the tart to cool for 10 minutes, then serve with ice cream or cream.

Fruit desserts

Baked saffron peaches with mango and cream

Preparation time **15 minutes**
Cooking time **15 minutes**
Serves **4**

2 large, slightly under-ripe peaches, halved and stoned
15 g (½ oz) pistachios, halved
a few saffron threads
a few drops of almond extract
30 g (1¼ oz) crunchy oat cereal
2 tablespoons orange juice
5-cm (2-inch) cinnamon stick, broken into 8 pieces

To serve
75 ml (3 fl oz) single cream
½ slightly under-ripe mango, thinly sliced
1 teaspoon grated plain dark chocolate (optional)

1 Scoop some of the peach out of the peach halves and chop this finely. Put the halved peaches, skin side down, in a lightly oiled baking dish.

2 Mix together the chopped peach flesh, pistachios, saffron, almond extract, oat cereal and orange juice. Spoon this mixture carefully into the peach halves.

3 Push the cinnamon stick pieces into the peach halves. Bake the peaches uncovered in a preheated oven, 180°C (350°F), Gas Mark 4, for 15 minutes.

4 Carefully arrange one peach half on each dessert plate and pour some of the cream over one side of the peach. Serve with mango slices and a sprinkling of chocolate, if using.

Hot berries with orange cream

Preparation time **15 minutes**
Cooking time **8 minutes**
Serves **4**

150 ml (¼ pint) reduced-fat
  Greek yogurt
125 ml (4 fl oz) single cream
1 egg yolk
1 teaspoon orange-blossom water
1 orange, peeled and pith removed,
  separated into segments
150 g (5 oz) blueberries
150 g (5 oz) strawberries, cut into
  bite-sized pieces

1 Mix together the yogurt, cream, egg yolk and orange-blossom water.

2 Mix the orange segments with the blueberries and strawberries. Put a mixture of each fruit in 4 ovenproof serving dishes and then spoon the sauce over to cover the fruit.

3 Place under a preheated hot grill for 5–8 minutes until the cream starts to bubble and turn brown.

4 Serve immediately, being sure to warn your guests about the hot dishes.

Mini almond angel cakes with berries

Preparation time **15 minutes**
Cooking time **10 minutes**
Serves **6**

oil, for greasing
4 egg whites
3 tablespoons granulated sweetener
50 g (2 oz) ground almonds
generous pinch of cream of tartar
15 g (½ oz) flaked almonds
400 g (13 oz) frozen mixed berries
200 g (7 oz) fromage frais
1 tablespoon sifted icing sugar, for
    dusting (optional)

1 Lightly oil 6 sections of a deep muffin tin and line the bases with circles of greaseproof paper.

2 Whisk the egg whites until stiff, moist peaks form. Whisk in the sweetener, a teaspoonful at a time, until it has all been added and continue to whisk for a minute or two until the mixture is thick and glossy.

3 Fold in the ground almonds and cream of tartar and spoon the mixture into the sections of the muffin tin. Sprinkle the flaked almonds over the top.

4 Cook in a preheated oven, 180°C (350°F), Gas Mark 4, for 10–12 minutes until golden brown and set. Loosen the edges of the cakes with a knife and lift them on to a wire rack.

5 Warm the berries in a saucepan. Arrange the angel cakes on serving plates, add a spoonful of fromage frais to each and spoon the berries around. Dust with a little sifted icing sugar, if using.

Roasted plums with ginger sauce

Preparation time **15 minutes**
Cooking time **15 minutes**
Serves **6**

625 g (1¼ lb) dessert plums
4 bay leaves
100 ml (3½ fl oz) white wine
2 tablespoons clear honey
50 g (2 oz) fresh root ginger
1 tablespoon caster sugar
75 ml (3 fl oz) water
150 g (5 oz) white chocolate,
　chopped
100 g (3½ oz) crème fraîche

1 Halve and stone the plums and arrange them in a single layer in a roasting tin or shallow ovenproof dish in which they fit snugly. Tuck the bay leaves around them.

2 Mix together the wine and honey and pour over the plums. Roast in a preheated oven, 220°C (425°F), Gas Mark 7, for 10–15 minutes or until the plums begin to colour but still retain their shape.

3 Grate the ginger and put it in a small heavy-based saucepan, scraping the gratings from the board and grater into the pan. Add the sugar and measured water. Heat gently, stirring until the sugar dissolves, then bring to the boil and boil for 1 minute. Strain into a clean pan.

4 Add the chopped chocolate to the pan and leave until melted, stirring frequently until smooth. If the chocolate doesn't melt, heat it through gently. Stir in the crème fraîche.

5 To serve, warm the sauce through gently. Transfer the plums to serving dishes, spoon over the cooking juices and serve with the sauce.

White chocolate and blueberry trifle

Preparation time **20 minutes**,
   plus chilling
Cooking time **2 minutes**
Serves **6–8**

600 ml (1 pint) milk
4 egg yolks
3 tablespoons cornflour
300 g (10 oz) white chocolate,
   chopped
300 g (10 oz) blueberries
4 tablespoons gin or vodka
4 tablespoons icing sugar, plus extra
   for dusting
300 g (10 oz) bought or homemade
   Madeira cake
300 ml (½ pint) double cream
2 tablespoons lemon juice
plain dark or white chocolate
   caraque, to decorate

1 To make the chocolate caraque, spread melted chocolate in a thin layer on a marble slab or a clean, smooth surface, such as a new, plastic chopping board or sturdy baking sheet. Leave to set. Holding a knife at an angle, draw it across the chocolate so that you scrape off curls. If the chocolate is too soft and doesn't curl, pop it in the refrigerator for a few minutes. If it is brittle and breaks off in thin shards, leave it for a while at room temperature before trying again.

2 Bring the milk almost to the boil in a medium-sized heavy-based saucepan. Beat together the egg yolks and cornflour in a bowl. Pour the milk over the yolks, stirring, then return the saucepan to the heat. Cook briefly until the mixture is thickened and bubbling. Stir in the chocolate until melted, and leave to cool.

3 Reserve 50 g (2 oz) of the blueberries. Pierce the remainder with a fork and add the gin or vodka and 2 tablespoons of the icing sugar. Stir, then leave for 5 minutes.

4 Cut the cake into chunks and scatter them in a large glass dish or individual dishes. Sprinkle with the soaked berries, then pile the cooled custard on top.

5 Whip the cream with the remaining icing sugar and the lemon juice until softly peaking. Spoon over the custard. Scatter with the reserved blueberries and chocolate caraque. Serve dusted with icing sugar.

Cranberry poached pears

Preparation time **10 minutes**, plus chilling

Cooking time **1 hour**

Serves **4**

475 ml (16 fl oz) cranberry juice
50 ml (2 fl oz) orange juice
125 g (4 oz) sugar
1 stick cinnamon
1 star anise (optional)
4 firm, ripe pears
125 g (4 oz) fresh cranberries

1 Put both juices and sugar in a saucepan big enough to hold the pears. Gently heat to dissolve the sugar. Add the cinnamon and star anise, if using, and boil for 5 minutes.

2 Peel the pears and immediately stand them in the pan with the cranberry syrup. Cover and simmer gently for 40 minutes, or until the pears are cooked and soft through to the centre when pierced with a skewer.

3 Remove from the heat and leave to cool completely in the syrup. Chill for 2 hours or overnight, occasionally turning the pears in the syrup to achieve an even colour.

4 Remove the pears from the pan and bring the cranberry syrup to the boil for 10 minutes, or until reduced to a thick syrup. Add the fresh cranberries and simmer for a further 5 minutes. Remove from the heat and set aside until completely cool.

5 Place the pears on a plate with the cranberries and pour the sauce over and around them.

Strawberry choux puffs

Preparation time **30 minutes**
Cooking time **30 minutes**
Makes **12**

50 g (2 oz) plain flour
50 g (2 oz) butter
2 eggs, beaten
1 teaspoon vanilla extract
300 g (10 oz) strawberries,
    thinly sliced
icing sugar, for dusting

Crème pâtissière
150 ml (5 fl oz) milk
150 ml (5 fl oz) double cream
1 vanilla pod
4 egg yolks
3 tablespoons caster sugar
2 tablespoons plain flour

1 Lightly grease a large baking sheet and sprinkle with water. Sift the flour onto a sheet of greaseproof paper. Cut the butter into pieces and melt it in a medium saucepan with 150 ml (¼ pint) water. Bring to the boil and take off the heat.

2 Tip in the flour and beat until the mixture forms a ball that comes away from the side of the pan. Leave to cool for 2 minutes, then gradually beat in the eggs until the mixture is smooth and glossy. Add the vanilla extract.

3 Place 12 even spoonfuls of mixture well apart on the baking sheet and bake in a preheated oven, 200°C (400°F), Gas Mark 6, for about 25 minutes until risen and golden. Make a slit around the middle of each and return them to the oven for 3 minutes to dry out. Cool on a wire rack.

4 To make the crème pâtissière, put the milk and cream into a medium heavy-based saucepan. Use the tip of a sharp knife to score the vanilla pod lengthways through to the centre. Add it to the pan and bring to the boil. Remove from the heat and let infuse for 20 minutes.

5 Beat together the egg yolks, sugar and flour until smooth. Remove the vanilla pod from the milk, scrape out the seeds with the tip of a knife and add them to the milk. Pour the milk over the egg mixture, beating well.

6 Return the custard to the pan and cook over a gentle heat, stirring constantly with a wooden spoon, for about 4–5 minutes until thick and smooth. Turn the custard into a small bowl and cover with waxed paper to prevent a skin from forming. Allow to cool before use.

7 Open out each puff and divide the sliced strawberries between them. Pile the crème pâtissière on top and push the puffs together. Dust with icing sugar and store in a cool place until ready to serve.

Figs with yogurt and honey

Preparation time **5 minutes**
Cooking time **10 minutes**
Serves **4**

8 ripe figs
4 tablespoons plain yogurt
2 tablespoons honey

1 Heat a grill pan under a medium heat and add the figs. Cook for 8 minutes, turning occasionally, until they are charred on the outside. Remove and cut in half.

2 Arrange the figs on 4 plates and serve with a spoonful of plain yogurt and some honey spooned over the top.

Spice-infused fruit salad

Preparation time **15 minutes**
Cooking time **2 minutes**
Serves **6**

1 vanilla pod
2½ tablespoons caster sugar
175 ml (6 fl oz) water
1 hot red chilli, halved and deseeded
4 clementines
2 peaches
½ cantaloupe melon, deseeded
100 g (3½ oz) blueberries
vanilla ice cream, to serve
   (optional)

1 Use the tip of a small, sharp knife to score the vanilla pod lengthways through to the centre. Heat the sugar in a medium saucepan with the measured water until the sugar dissolves. Add the vanilla pod and chilli and heat gently for 2 minutes. Remove the pan from the heat and leave to cool slightly.

2 Cut away the zest from the clementines and slice the flesh. Stone and slice the peaches. Cut the melon flesh into small chunks, discarding the skin.

3 Mix the fruits in a serving dish and pour over the warm syrup, discarding the chilli. Let the syrup cool completely, then cover the fruit salad and chill until you are ready to serve. Serve with vanilla ice cream, if liked.

Hazelnut and pear roulade with mascarpone

Preparation time **30 minutes**,
   plus cooling
Cooking time **18–19 minutes**
Serves **6–8**

125 g (4 oz) hazelnuts
5 eggs, separated
175 g (6 oz) caster sugar, plus extra
   for sprinkling
1 just-ripe pear, peeled and
   coarsely grated

Filling
200 g (7 oz) mascarpone cheese
2 tablespoons icing sugar
250 g (8 oz) fresh apricots, stoned
   and roughly chopped (or tinned
   apricots, drained)

1 Line a 23 x 30-cm (9 x 12-inch) roasting tin with baking paper and cut into the corners so the paper fits snugly.

2 Put the hazelnuts on a piece of foil and toast under the grill for 3–4 minutes until golden. Roughly chop 2 tablespoons and set aside for decoration, then grind the remainder in a liquidizer or food processor until very finely chopped.

3 Whisk the egg yolks and caster sugar in a large bowl until thick and pale, and the whisk leaves a trail when lifted above the mixture. Fold the toasted finely chopped hazelnuts and grated pear into the egg yolk mixture.

4 Wash the whisk and dry it well, then use it to whisk the egg whites into stiff, moist-looking peaks. Fold a large spoonful into the nut mixture to loosen it, then gently fold in the remaining egg whites.

5 Spoon the mixture into the prepared tin and ease it into the corners. Bake the roulade in a preheated oven, 180°C (350°F), Gas Mark 4, for 15 minutes until it is well risen, golden brown and the top feels spongy. Cover with a clean tea towel and leave to cool for at least 1 hour.

6 Beat the mascarpone and icing sugar together until soft. Wet a clean tea towel, wring out and place on the work surface so that a short edge is nearest you. Cover with a large piece of baking paper and sprinkle with a little caster sugar. Turn the cooled roulade out on to the paper, remove the tin and peel away the lining paper.

7 Spread the roulade with the mascarpone mixture, then sprinkle with apricots. Roll up the roulade, starting from the shortest side nearest you, using the sugared paper and tea towel. Transfer to a serving plate, sprinkle with chopped hazelnuts and cut into thick slices to serve.

Drunken orange slices

Preparation time **10 minutes**
Cooking time **12 minutes**
Serves **4**

4 large sweet oranges
50 ml (2 fl oz) cold water
65 g (2½ oz) muscovado sugar
3 tablespoons Cointreau
2 tablespoons whisky
juice of 1 small orange
1 vanilla pod, split lengthways
1 cinnamon stick
4 cloves
2–3 mace blades (optional)
ginger ice cream, to serve

1 Using a small, sharp knife, cut off the base and the top of each orange. Now cut down around the curve of the orange to remove all the peel and pith, leaving just the orange flesh. Cut the flesh horizontally into 5-mm (¼-inch) slices and set aside.

2 In a small saucepan, very gently heat the water, sugar, 2 tablespoons of the Cointreau, the whisky, orange juice, vanilla pod, cinnamon stick, cloves and mace until the sugar has dissolved. Now turn up the heat and boil rapidly for 5 minutes. Cool slightly, but keep warm.

3 Heat a grill pan over a high heat, then quickly grill the orange slices for 1 minute on each side until caramelized. Top the syrup with the remaining Cointreau and set alight. Once the flames have died down, arrange the orange slices on serving dishes and drizzle with the flamed syrup.

4 Serve the orange slices immediately with the ginger ice cream, or an ice cream of your choice.

Baked ricotta cheesecake with poached plums

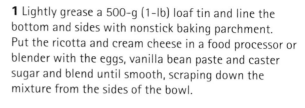

Preparation time **20 minutes**
Cooking time **40 minutes**
Serves **6**

500 g (1 lb) ricotta cheese
300 g (10 oz) cream cheese
2 eggs
2 teaspoons vanilla bean paste
125 g (4 oz) caster sugar

Poached plums
½ small orange
1 teaspoon whole cloves
2 tablespoons dark
   muscovado sugar
1 cinnamon stick
175 ml (6 fl oz) water
375 g (12 oz) red plums, halved
   and stoned
2 tablespoons redcurrant jelly

1 Lightly grease a 500-g (1-lb) loaf tin and line the bottom and sides with nonstick baking parchment. Put the ricotta and cream cheese in a food processor or blender with the eggs, vanilla bean paste and caster sugar and blend until smooth, scraping down the mixture from the sides of the bowl.

2 Transfer the mixture to the loaf tin and put it in a small roasting tin. Pour hot water into the pan to a depth of 2.5 cm (1 inch) and bake the cheesecake in a preheated oven, 160°C (325°F), Gas Mark 3, for about 40 minutes until it is lightly set. Lift the cheesecake out of the water and leave to cool in the loaf tin.

3 Meanwhile, poach the plums. Stud the orange with the cloves and put it in a heavy-bottomed saucepan with the muscovado sugar, cinnamon stick and the measured water. Bring the water to the boil, then reduce the heat and add the plums. Cover the pan and cook the plums very gently for about 5 minutes or until they are just tender. (The cooking time will vary depending on the type of plum used.)

4 Lift out the plums and add the redcurrant jelly to the pan. Bring the liquid to the boil and boil for about 2 minutes until it is reduced and syrupy. Remove the orange and cinnamon stick and pour the syrup over the plums. Leave the syrup to cool, then chill the plums until you are ready to serve.

5 Remove the cheesecake from the tin and peel away the lining paper. Serve it in slices, topped with the poached plums.

Something special

Zabaglione with Champagne

Preparation time **10 minutes**
Cooking time **15 minutes**
Serves **4**

300 ml (½ pint) Champagne or Cava
1 egg
5 egg yolks
150 g (5 oz) caster sugar
grated rind of 2 lemons

Tuiles
1 egg white
65 g (2½ oz) caster sugar
50 g (2 oz) plain flour
50 g (2 oz) butter, melted
5 strawberries, cut into small dice

fresh strawberries, to serve

1 To make the tuiles, grease and flour 2 baking sheets. Beat the egg white until frothy, then add the sugar, flour and butter and stir until well mixed.

2 For each tuile, spoon 2 teaspoons of the mixture on to a prepared baking sheet. Sprinkle with a little diced strawberry and bake in a preheated oven at 200°C (400°F), Gas Mark 6, for 8–10 minutes or until golden.

3 Remove the tuiles from the oven and while they are still hot place them over a rolling pin. Leave until set, then cool on a wire rack.

4 To make the zabaglione, pour the Champagne into a saucepan and boil rapidly until reduced to 125 ml (4 fl oz). Set aside to cool. Place the egg and egg yolks in a heatproof bowl with the sugar and whisk until doubled in volume.

5 Place the bowl over a pan of gently simmering water, add the reduced Champagne and lemon rind and whisk for about 8 minutes, until the mixture is very thick and creamy. Serve the zabaglione immediately in a bowl or in individual glasses surrounded by tuiles and some fresh strawberries.

Cardamom and coconut syllabub with almond brittle

Preparation time **15 minutes**,
  plus chilling
Cooking time **about 10 minutes**
Serves **4**

Brittle
50 g (2 oz) sugar
25 g (1 oz) flaked almonds, toasted

Syllabub
200 ml (7 fl oz) coconut cream
300 ml (½ pint) double cream
15 cardamom seeds, lightly crushed
2 tablespoons caster sugar

1 Make the brittle. Put the sugar and almonds in a saucepan over a low heat. While the sugar melts, lightly oil a baking sheet. When the sugar has melted and turned golden, pour the mixture on to the baking sheet and set it aside to cool. (The brittle can be made a day or two in advance and stored in an airtight container.)

2 Pour the coconut cream and double cream into a large bowl. Add the crushed cardamom seeds and caster sugar, then whisk these ingredients together until lightly whipped and just holding soft peaks.

3 Spoon the syllabub into 4 glasses and chill. Meanwhile, lightly crack the brittle into irregular shards. When ready to serve, top the syllabub with the brittle.

Ricotta and chocolate trifle

Preparation time **15 minutes**,
  plus chilling
Serves **4**

100 g (3½ oz) almond biscotti
75 ml (3 fl oz) orange juice
1 tablespoon brandy (optional)
200 g (7 oz) ricotta cheese
150 g (5 oz) reduced-fat
  Greek yogurt
3 tablespoons icing sugar
few drops of vanilla extract
25 g (1 oz) plain dark chocolate,
  minimum 70 per cent cocoa
  solids, grated
100 g (3½ oz) blueberries

1 Soak the biscotti in the orange juice and brandy, if using.

2 Meanwhile, beat the ricotta together with the Greek yogurt, icing sugar and vanilla extract until smooth and creamy.

3 Spoon the soaked biscotti into the base of 4 glass sundae dishes. Divide half the cheese mixture among the glasses. Top with half the grated chocolate and then the blueberries. Spoon the remaining cheese mixture into the dishes and finish with a semicircle of grated chocolate. Chill for at least 30 minutes before serving.

Zucotto

Preparation time **25 minutes**,
   plus chilling
Serves **6–8**

350 g (11½ oz) bought or
   homemade chocolate
   sponge cake
350 ml (12 fl oz) double cream
4 tablespoons maraschino liqueur
   or brandy
40 g (1½ oz) icing sugar, plus extra
   for dusting
75 g (3 oz) plain dark chocolate,
   chopped
50 g (2 oz) whole sweet almonds,
   toasted and chopped
50 g (2 oz) unblanched hazelnuts,
   toasted and chopped
75 g (3 oz) natural glacé
   cherries, halved
cocoa powder, for dusting

1 Thinly slice the chocolate cake. Line a 1.8-litre (3-pint)
bowl with clingfilm (it's best to use a mixing bowl with a
round base rather than a flat base). Use about two-
thirds of the cake to line the bowl in a single layer,
cutting it to fit neatly together. The lining should come
about two-thirds of the way up the sides of the bowl.

2 Put the cream, the liqueur or brandy and the icing
sugar in a bowl and whisk until just peaking. Stir in the
chocolate, nuts and cherries. Spoon the mixture into the
cake-lined bowl, spreading it in an even layer.

3 Use the remaining cake and any excess cake lining the
bowl to cover the top of the filling. Cover the bowl with
clingfilm and chill overnight.

4 Invert the cake on to a plate and peel away the
clingfilm. Cut 4 wedge-shaped templates from paper.
Dust the cake with icing sugar and lay the templates
over the top with their points meeting in the centre to
make a sunburst pattern. Dust between the paper with
cocoa powder, then carefully lift away the paper.

Petites crémets with lavender and strawberries

Preparation time **20 minutes**, plus chilling

Serves **6**

1 egg white
150 ml (¼ pint) double cream
150 g (5 oz) fromage frais
100 g (3½ oz) low-fat
    natural yogurt
4 teaspoons clear honey
2–3 lavender flowers, plus extra
    for decoration
400 g (13 oz) strawberries, hulled

1 Cut 6 squares of muslin, 18 cm (7 inches) square, and use them to line 6 ramekin dishes. Whip the egg white until stiffly peaking. Without washing the whisk, whip the cream until it is softly peaking.

2 Fold the fromage frais, yogurt and honey into the cream. Tear the flowers from the lavender stems and fold them into the cream mixture with the egg white.

3 Divide the mixture among the muslin-lined dishes. Bring the edges of the muslin together and tie them with string. Lift the muslin bundles out of the dishes and place them on a wire rack set over a plate or baking sheet to catch the drips. Chill for 4 hours or overnight.

4 Mash the strawberries with a fork. Remove the muslin and string from the crémets and place each in the centre of a serving plate. Spoon the strawberries around and decorate with lavender flowers.

Peach and almond roulade

Preparation time **20 minutes**,
  plus chilling
Cooking time **20 minutes**
Serves **8**

butter, for greasing
125 g (4 oz) white almond paste
5 eggs, separated
125 g (4 oz) caster sugar, plus extra
  for dusting
3 tablespoons plain flour
2 tablespoons brandy or
  almond liqueur
2 ripe peaches
300 g (10 oz) crème fraîche

1 Grease and line a 33 x 23-cm (13 x 9-inch) Swiss roll tin with baking paper. Grease the paper. Grate the almond paste.

2 Whisk the egg yolks in a bowl with the sugar until pale and creamy. Whisk in the almond paste. Stir in the flour.

3 In a separate, thoroughly clean bowl whisk the egg whites until peaking. Use a large metal spoon to fold the egg whites into the almond mixture until combined. Turn the mixture into the tin and spread it gently into the corners.

4 Bake in a preheated oven, 180°C (350°F), Gas Mark 4, for 20 minutes or until risen and firm to the touch. Sprinkle a sheet of baking parchment with sugar and invert the roulade on to it. Leave to cool.

5 Drizzle the brandy or liqueur over the sponge. Thinly slice the peaches. Spread the crème fraîche over the sponge and scatter with the peaches. Starting at a thin end, roll up the roulade and transfer to a serving plate. Chill until ready to serve.

Chocolate mousse cake with Amaretto cream

Preparation time **30 minutes**
Cooking time **30–35 minutes**
Serves **8**

250 g (8 oz) plain dark chocolate,
   broken into pieces
125 g (4 oz) unsalted butter, diced
5 eggs, separated
3 tablespoons semi-skimmed milk
4 tablespoons granulated sweetener
1 teaspoon vanilla extract

Amaretto cream
150 ml (¼ pint) whipping cream
100 g (3½ oz) fromage frais
2 tablespoons Amaretto liqueur

sifted cocoa and chocolate curls
   (see page 10), to decorate

1 Put the chocolate and butter in a saucepan and heat gently until melted. Meanwhile, line the base and sides of a 23-cm (9-inch) springform tin with nonstick baking paper. Take the chocolate pan off the heat and stir in the egg yolks, milk, sweetener and vanilla.

2 Whisk the egg whites until stiff, moist peaks form. Fold a tablespoon into the chocolate mixture to loosen it slightly, then fold in the remainder.

3 Pour the mixture into the tin. Bake in a preheated oven, 180°C (350°F), Gas Mark 4, for 30–35 minutes until well risen and the centre is still slightly spongy. Leave to cool in the tin. (The cake sinks on cooling.)

4 Whip the cream and fold in the fromage frais and liqueur. Serve with a slice of cake dusted with a little sifted cocoa and sprinkled with chocolate curls.

Eton mess

Preparation time **20 minutes**,
plus chilling
Cooking time **1 hour**
Serves **6**

2 egg whites
100 g (3½ oz) caster sugar
200 g (7 oz) Greek yogurt
350 g (11½ oz) fresh raspberries

White chocolate ganache
150 ml (¼ pint) double cream
150 g (5 oz) white chocolate,
chopped

1 Line a large baking sheet with nonstick baking paper. Whisk the egg whites in a clean bowl until stiff. Gradually whisk in the sugar, a tablespoonful at a time, whisking well after each addition, until the meringue is stiff and glossy. Put spoonfuls on the baking sheet and bake in a preheated oven, 140°C (275°F), Gas Mark 1, for about 1 hour until crisp. Transfer to a wire rack and leave to cool.

2 To make the ganache, put half the cream in a medium-sized heavy-based saucepan and heat gently until it is bubbling around the edges. Remove from the heat and stir in the chopped chocolate. Leave to stand for a few minutes until the chocolate has melted, then stir lightly and turn into a bowl. Chill for 15 minutes until cool.

3 Add the remaining cream to the bowl and then whisk with a hand-held electric mixer until the ganache just starts to hold its shape. Don't overwhisk or it will start to separate.

4 Mix together the ganache and yogurt. Take 75 g (3 oz) of the meringues (keep the rest in an airtight container) and crumble them into a large bowl. If they're a bit sticky in the centre, just pull them apart. Stir in the raspberries.

5 Add the ganache mixture and lightly fold the ingredients together. Spoon into 6 glasses and chill until ready to serve.

Chocolate Amaretto jellies

Preparation time **15 minutes**,
plus setting
Cooking time **5 minutes**
Serves **8**

1 tablespoon powdered gelatine
3 tablespoons water
300 g (10 oz) plain dark chocolate,
broken up
150 ml (¼ pint) Amaretto liqueur
450 ml (¾ pint) milk
100 ml (3½ fl oz) double cream

Glossy chocolate syrup
25 g (1 oz) caster sugar
150 ml (¼ pint) water
50 g (2 oz) plain dark chocolate,
chopped

1 Sprinkle the gelatine over 3 tablespoons water in a small bowl and leave to soak for 5 minutes. Melt the chocolate in a large bowl with the liqueur, stirring frequently until smooth.

2 Bring the milk just to the boil and remove from the heat. Pour the warm milk over the chocolate, whisking well until completely smooth.

3 Add the soaked gelatine and stir for 1 minute until dissolved. Divide among 8 125–150 ml (4–5 fl oz) individual moulds and leave to cool. Chill for at least 6 hours, preferably overnight, until just firm.

4 To make the glossy chocolate syrup, put the sugar in a small heavy-based saucepan with the measured water and heat gently, stirring until the sugar dissolves. Bring to the boil and boil for 1 minute. Remove from the heat and stir in the chocolate. Leave until melted, then reheat gently until the syrup is smooth and glossy. Turn the syrup into a small jug, ready for pouring.

5 To serve, half-fill a small bowl with very hot water and dip a mould up to the rim in the water for 2 seconds. Invert on to a serving plate and, gripping both plate and mould, shake the jelly out on the plate. Lift away the mould and repeat with the other jellies.

6 Pour a little cream around each jelly, then drizzle a tablespoonful of syrup through it. Lightly swirl the syrup into the cream to decorate.

Vanilla bean crème brûlée

Preparation time **20 minutes**,
plus chilling
Cooking time **25–30 minutes**
Serves **6**

1 vanilla pod
600 ml (1 pint) double cream
8 egg yolks
50 g (2 oz) caster sugar
3 tablespoons icing sugar
raspberries, strawberries and mint
leaves, to serve (optional)

1 Slit the vanilla pod lengthways and put it in a saucepan. Pour the cream into the pan, then bring almost to the boil. Take off the heat and leave to stand for 15 minutes for the vanilla flavour to develop.

2 Lift the vanilla pod out of the cream and, holding it against the side of the saucepan, scrape the black seeds into the cream. Discard the pod casing.

3 Use a fork to mix together the egg yolks and caster sugar in a bowl. Reheat the cream, then gradually mix it into the eggs and sugar. Strain the mixture back into the saucepan.

4 Place 6 ovenproof ramekins or custard cups in a roasting tin, then divide the custard between them. Pour warm water around the dishes to come halfway up the sides, then bake in a preheated oven at 180°C (350°F), Gas Mark 4, for 20–25 minutes until the custards are just set with a slight softness at the centre.

5 Leave the dishes to cool in the water, then lift them out and chill in the refrigerator for 3–4 hours. About 25 minutes before serving, sprinkle the tops with icing sugar (no need to sift). Caramelize using a blowtorch, then leave at room temperature. Serve by itself or with raspberries, strawberries and mint leaves dusted with icing sugar.

Florentine vanilla cheesecake

Preparation time **25 minutes**
Cooking time **45 minutes**
Serves **8–10**

125 g (4 oz) plain dark chocolate
30 g (1¼ oz) flaked almonds,
   lightly toasted
2½ tablespoons mixed peel,
   finely chopped
6 glacé cherries, finely chopped
75 g (3 oz) digestive biscuits,
   crushed
50 g (2 oz) unsalted butter, melted

Filling
500 g (1 lb) cream cheese
2 teaspoons vanilla bean paste
150 ml (¼ pint) double cream
150 ml (¼ pint) Greek yogurt
125 g (4 oz) caster sugar
3 eggs

1 Grease a 20-cm (8-inch) loose-bottomed cake tin and line the sides with a strip of nonstick baking parchment. Chop half the chocolate into small pieces, reserving the remainder for decoration. Lightly crush the almonds and mix them in a bowl with the chopped chocolate, mixed peel, glacé cherries, biscuit crumbs and butter. Stir the mixture until well combined, then transfer it to the cake tin, packing it into the bottom and slightly up the sides to form a shell.

2 Make the filling. Beat the cream cheese and vanilla bean paste in a bowl until smooth. Beat in the cream, yogurt, sugar and eggs to make a smooth batter.

3 Pour the egg mixture into the tin and bake in a preheated oven, 160°C (325°F), Gas Mark 3, for about 45 minutes or until the surface feels just firm around the edges but is still very wobbly in the centre. Turn off the heat and leave the cheesecake to cool in the oven.

4 Transfer the cheesecake to a serving plate and peel away the lining paper. Melt the remaining chocolate and use a teaspoon to drizzle the chocolate around the top edges of the cheesecake. Chill until ready to serve.

Index

Acknowledgements

Executive Editor: Nicola Hill
Senior Editor: Lisa John
Executive Art Editor: Penny Stock
Design: Ginny Zeal
Senior Production Controller: Manjit Sihra
Picture Library Assistant: Ciaran O'Reilly

All photography © Octopus Publishing Group
Limited /Emma Neish 7, 77; /Gareth Sambridge
100, 104; /Gus Filgate 52; /Ian Wallace 83; /Jeremy
Hopley 109, 123; /Lis Parsons 2, 37, 38, 39, 43, 44,
46, 48, 51, 67, 84, 86, 91, 92, 101, 102, 113, 117,
125; /Philip Webb 80, 97; /Stephen Conroy 15, 16,
19, 20, 21, 23, 25, 26, 27, 28, 30, 31, 33, 34, 54,
58, 60, 62, 64, 68, 70, 71, 72, 74, 79, 93, 94, 96,
110, 115, 116, 119, 120, 121.